In His Glory,

I Learned to

Lean on God

McDougal & Associates
Servants of Christ and Stewards of the
Mysteries of God

In His Glory, I Learned to Lean on God

Battling AUTISM Through God's Word

by

Patricia A. Lee

Published by:

McDougal & Associates
18896 Greenwell Springs Road
Greenwell Springs, LA 70739
www.thepublishedword.com

McDougal & Associates is dedicated to the spreading of the Gospel of Jesus Christ to as many people as possible in the shortest time possible.

ISBN 978-1-934769-47-8

Printed in the US, the UK and Australia
For Worldwide Distribution

Dedication

I would like to dedicate this book to my youngest son, **Grady Devon Lee**. God said:

> *Before I formed thee in the belly I knew thee; and before thou camest forth out of the womb I sanctified thee, and I ordained thee a prophet unto the nations.*   Jeremiah 1:5

Grady, I carried you for nine months under my heart, and then I have raised you the past twenty-eight years with that same heart. My dearest son, I love you so much. You have been chosen by the hand of God to reach out and help others. Through many years of trials and tribulations, you have suffered. My heart has been in sorrow to see the suffering and sacrifices you have gone through. But through it all, I put you in the Master's hand, and what a wonderful masterpiece He has created! He has recreated you as one who is whole, with nothing missing and nothing broken. God has great things for you, my son. Now go ye into all the world, and preach the Gospel to every creature:

> *And thou shalt love the* LORD *thy God with all*
> *thine heart, and with all thy soul, and with all*
> *thy might.* Deuteronomy 6:5

And all will go well with thee.

Your Loving Mother,
Patricia A. Lee

Second Dedication

(My love letter to my heavenly Father)

Father God, my Lord, and Savior Jesus Christ, I thank You for Your great love You have shown me in my great tribulation period. I worship You and adore You for being *"I Am that I Am" from Genesis to Revelation.* You have been Grady's Jehovah, his father (Genesis 2:7); his Jehovah Jireh, his Provider (Genesis 22:8); his Jehovah Nissi, his Victory (Exodus 17:15); his Jehovah Shalom, his peace (Judges 6:24); and his Jehovah Rophe, his Healer (Exodus 15:26). God, You are my love, and I love You so much. When I felt that I was slipping, you were my Solid Rock to hold on to. When my body and mind were tired, You were my goodness and my Fortress, my High Tower, and my Deliverer, my Shield in whom I trust.

You remind me of the poem about the footprints in the sand, for You have carried me when I needed You the most. I dedicate my life to You, Father, for You not only have carried me, but You have also supported me and, most of all, You have chosen me for this anointing for a time such as this, to help Your people, and I'm grateful and humbled to be Your servant, looking one day to see Your glorious face.

Your Daughter and Servant,
With Everlasting Love,
Patricia A. Lee

Acknowledgments

I would like to give praise and glory to my heavenly Father for making this book possible. Father, You have truly been a blessing to me. Thank You, Father God, with everlasting love.

Father, through the years You have truly blessed me through special people with special and unique gifts and talents. I say to each one of them, Thank you from the bottom of my heart. I couldn't have done this without you. God selected you for this particular season in my life, and may He richly bless each one of you.

Thanks to all of Grady's bus drivers for your love, efforts and carefulness in transporting him to school and home again. Thanks to all the wonderful teachers for assisting in every area of his development. What a wonderful job you have done! Thanks to all the loving caregivers for your labors of love: Edward Terry, Linda Caughman and Terry Taylor.

My sister, Linda Caughman, departed from this world on October 30, 2010 before this book was published. I owe a special thanks to her for assisting with Grady. I love her much now and always.

Thanks to a caring, loving, dedicated school psychology director from Richland District 2, Patty Gandy. I give special thanks to Grady's psychiatrist at Baptist Hospital, Dr. Timothy D. Malone, for his support, love, devotion and endurance.

Thanks to my special friends, for supporting me when needed: Minister Cathy Harris and Anthony Griffen.

I thank God for Pastor Ernest and Sylvia Bostic and family and for their great love and support in every area where is has been needed.

Thanks, Edwin Jackson, for being a loving service coordinator who supported Grady through six years of services. You were dedicated, loving and went beyond the call of duty.

I thank God for my photographer, Willie Mullins of JWE Photography of Columbia, South Carolina.

Thanks to Grady's loving relatives who are always there to be a blessing, Uncle Willie and Louise Brown, and to my loving parents for their support: Grady and Lula B. Wise.

Special thanks to my magnificent sons, Cornelious Lee and Adolphus Lee, Ill. Thank you for your great love and faithfulness. You have been my pillars to help hold my ministry together. You are blessed and highly favored. You have fought a good fight. Mother love will always remember your loyalty. Well done, my faithful sons.

Contents

About the Title

When this book went into production in early 2011, my publisher called me one day to say that he felt the title did not agree with the text of the book. It was, he said, in the difficult trials or storms of life that I had learned to lean on God. I understood where he was coming from, but I had to respectfully disagree. I knew that if it had not been for the glory of God that permeated my life on a daily basis during those most difficult trials, Grady would have been institutionalized a long time ago or I would have or both of us. God's glory surrounding us enabled us to hold on until the end, trusting God at every difficult turn of the road.

To some, our situation may have seemed hopeless or desperate beyond endurance. The book was written to help the many Christians who have given up on God. They prayed, and they stood on His Word, and still the storms rage about them, so that they have lost faith. This story should prove to them that God never fails. Rather, it is our faith that fails. Hold fast! Your victory is coming too.

Patricia Lee

Publisher's Foreword

Autism in one of those words any parent dreads to hear. It is a very strange malady, appearing in children, usually before the age of three, and one that, so far, at least, provides little hope of recovery. There is not yet any known cause and not yet any known cure. It is reported that approximately 9 out of every 1,000 children in the United States are diagnosed with this disorder, and this number has been increasing since the 1980s. No one is sure if this is due to better diagnostic techniques or whether there is an actual increase in cases.

What exactly is autism? In clinical terms autism is defined as "a disorder of neural development characterized by impaired social interaction and communication, and by restricted and repetitive behavior." Some autistic children seem to grow normally at first and then regress. Not many children with autism live independently after reaching adulthood, though some do become successful.

There are several things we can say for sure that relate to the testimony of this book:

- Having an autistic child is a burden, one that many parents find simply unbearable.
- Having an autistic child demands great resources of wisdom, compassion, patience and perseverance.
- When an autistic child is healed, it is a miracle that no one can deny.

This, then, is a story that should give hope to any mother and father, brother and sister. God is able.

Harold McDougal
Publisher

Introduction

This is the testimony of my twenty-eight-year-old son, Grady, who was diagnosed at the age of three and a half with autism. I have been through many storms in life, but this was a turbulent one that shook me in every respect. The foundation that had been set for my life had to be shored up by the Holy Ghost, or I could not have stood, but this storm had a purpose and was to prepare me (and my son) for ministry. That ministry is to help others, through faith, know how to weather the storms that may assail their own lives.

I know where my help cometh from, and it cometh from the Lord. I know my Healer, and He is my God

(Jehovah Rophe). Because my God is able to do exceeding abundantly above all that we ask or think, according to the power that worketh in us, I have asked Him to allow the words of this book to be an inspiration to everyone who reads it.

So sit back and let the power of God take you on a journey, as you read *In His Glory, I Learned to Lean on God!*

Patricia A. Lee
Columbia, South Carolina

Chapter 1

Battling Autism through God's Word

TRUSTING GOD IN EVERYTHING

When Grady Lee was born, on June 4, 1982, he seemed to be a healthy baby boy. His father and I had asked God, before his conception, for a girl, but God gave me just what I needed. He said:

> *For your Father knoweth what things ye have need of, before ye ask Him.* Matthew 6:8

When Grady was just fifteen months old, he received a prophetic word from our pastor. The word was that the devil would try to take his life. That pastor was a true prophet. His name was Elder C.D. McNeil, and he was from Fayetteville, North Carolina. A powerful man of God, he was my spiritual father, and I loved him very much. Unfortunately, he died in 1985 and went on to be with the Lord.

From the very beginning, the devil feared Grady because at a very young age he was full of the Spirit of God. One Sunday, after leaving a particularly blessed service, his father carried him into the house and set him down on the floor, and Grady began dancing in the Spirit, praising God, and this continued for about fifteen minutes. His daddy and I watched him spellbound. I knew, from that moment on, that Grady had a great destiny in God.

When he was just a year and a half old, I came to realize that Grady had a prophet's eyes. He would point, indicating things that he could see that the rest of us could not.

However, there were also unexplained negative elements in Grady's development. Although he felt secure in his mother's arms, for instance, he always seemed to be looking around with fear on his face. Then one day I had Grady in a McDonald's restaurant, and he suddenly got out of his seat and ran for the door.

When it became obvious that something was seriously wrong with Grady, we took him to a series of specialists to be tested. He was, by then, three and a half, and yet his motor skills had not developed to the level of a three year old. After eight hours of testing, our beloved son was diagnosed with autism and ADHD. In later years, he was also diagnosed with a profound range of mental retardation and adaptive behavioral problems.

I WON'T LOSE FAITH

You can imagine how difficult all of this was for us, but we faced it with faith in God. When the doctors diagnosed Grady as autistic, I diagnosed him as healed, for God has said in His Word:

Now faith is the substance of things hoped for, the evidence of things not seen.

Hebrews 11:1

As always, we were determined to trust God and give Grady's condition totally over to Him. His Word declares:

Now unto him that is able to do exceeding abundantly above all that we ask or think, according to the power that worketh in us.

Ephesians 3:20

Our hope was in God.

Grady developed into a very shy and quiet child. Autism denies a child the proper social skills to interact with others, and he would play with his toys all alone for hours at a time. When he wanted something, he would never ask for it, only point. But, with everything, he was Mama's Little Man, and I took very special care of him and showed him how much he was loved.

After his diagnosis, Grady started school very young, in an attempt to get a jump on the things that threatened his life. He was still very much Mama's Baby Boy, but now he had to get on the school bus every morning at 7:00 A.M. That's very hard for any child not yet four years old. But at that tender age, Grady began attending regular kindergarten classes.

It was so touching to see him trying to climb the bus steps with his short legs. Then he would find a seat as close as possible to a window so that he could stare out at Mama, with those big brown eyes, as the bus pulled away. I can remember it as if it was just yesterday. It was still dark outside, the bus had its lights on, and it was backing out of our driveway with Mama's Baby Boy onboard. What emotions I felt in those moments!

From the minute we received those test results, our lives were changed forever. Someone had to be with Grady at all times, and this didn't change as he got older. Age didn't seem to make a difference with autism. At every level, Grady still had to have assistance in bathing and with all of his personal hygiene. Still, I knew in my heart that his life was in the Master's hands. God declares the end from the beginning:

> *Only I can tell you the future before it even happens.* Isaiah 46:10, NLT

Whatever came, we would trust our God.

ONE STEP AT A TIME

When anyone talked to Grady, he was able to understand what they were saying, but usually he would not respond. If he did, it was with only a few words. When we were in Germany (because his father was in the military) his teacher said that one day he suddenly looked up and said, "Sky." Until then, she hadn't known that he could talk. Later she heard him say "French fries." That's how little he spoke.

As often happens with families struck by autism, when Grady was just six, I suddenly found myself raising him alone. I was now a single parent, and there were two older brothers. Cornelious was sixteen at the time, and Adolphus was nine. It was a scary time. Alone, with three sons to care for and one of them requiring such specialized attention, I faced a very uncertain future. But my faith was in God. He would not fail me.

By now Grady had started acting out in school, and I had to be prepared to go get him at any time, because I never knew when his teacher might call. She was doing her best, but she just couldn't handle him sometimes. The problem was that Grady didn't want to sit down when it was time to sit down, and he didn't want to behave when he was told to, and that was just the beginning. He started having other, more serious, behavioral problems.

For one things, he started running away from whoever was caring for him at the time, me included. He would jump out of the car as soon as it stopped and then run into the road as fast as he could. I was standing at the register at a store at the

Fort Jackson Shopping Center one day when he suddenly ran out of the store and directly into the road. Like any parent, I was alarmed, but I also knew that God kept Grady's personal guardian angels with him at all times. That day every car stopped immediately, and Grady was unhurt. God's promise is:

> *For he shall give his angles charge over thee, to*
> *keep thee in all thy ways.*   Psalm 91:11

As Grady became a faster runner, he had to be watched carefully at all times. Eventually he became so fast that no one could catch him on foot. If he got out, we had to jump in the car in order to overcome him and bring him back. I wondered if we might not need to let him try out for the Olympics. His legs had such strength, and he ran with such determination.

I'M YOUR HEALER, JEHOVAH ROPHE

Then, around the age of eight, Grady started having periods of uncontrolled rage. These became so severe that, at the tender age of nine, he was out of control and had to be hospitalized for several weeks. I cried, for it was the first time I had been separated from my baby boy, and Grady cried too. I had been admitted to a hospital before, but I had never had to leave Grady alone with strangers. Now I visited him every day ... until his doctors asked me not to. Grady was not adjusting to his environment, they said.

I asked them not to wash Grady's clothes. I wanted to do that myself. I would pick up his dirty laundry every week and leave fresh, nicely-starched and pressed shirts and pants in exchange. I also gave Grady his regular haircuts. I did this every time he was hospitalized. I had been cutting his hair since he was a year old, and only I could do it (because he would frequently experience one of his rages when anyone tried to cut his hair). It was an ordeal, and before I could finish, my clothes were soaked with perspiration.

Now, sadly, Grady was put on some serious medications. The doctors first tried Ritalin, and when that didn't seem to help him, they tried others. I wasn't happy about him being on medications because we had always trusted Jesus as our Great Physician, and He had never failed us. I cried out to Him as the medical team experimented with one drug after another, and none of them could seem to calm my son.

After Grady had come home, one day I went into the bathroom and found that he had feces all over the walls. The medications they were experimenting with were not agreeing with his system.

We went through several doctors during this period. A mother who loves her son needs to know that his doctor does too. When one doctor could not seem to bring Grady under control, we would try another one. Something had to be done. My son, whom I loved with all my heart, was slipping away from us.

Chapter 2

There Is Peace, Love and the Power of God in the Midst of the Storm

I WILL NEVER LEAVE YOU NOR FORSAKE YOU

From the time he was born, Grady always went to church with us, but as the years passed and he became more and more violent, we eventually had to stop taking him. The last time he went he hit a man in the head. At the time, I hadn't learned how to control this behavior. In time I learned that the Word of God was powerful enough for this too. When you work the Word of God, the Word of God will work for you:

> *For the word of God is quick, and powerful, and sharper than any twoedged sword, piercing even to the dividing asunder of soul and spirit, and of the joints and marrow, and is a discerner of the thoughts and intents of the heart.*
>
> Hebrews 4:12

That summer, Grady went to stay with his paternal grandmother in Cleveland, Ohio, as he did several summers. While he was there that year, a family member took him to a friend's house. There Grady picked up a cigarette lighter and set the bedroom on fire, and they had to call the fire department. He was sent home to me immediately.

On another occasion, while visiting his aunt there in Cleveland, Grady left the house without anyone noticing and went to McDonald's by himself. This happened when he was still quite young, but I just learned about it this past year.

Grady has always had his angels protecting him,

and this time was no different. And, on this occasion, he also proved how smart he was. He decided to sit with some children who were celebrating a birthday party, and what better way to get a free meal? No one seemed to mind that he had invited himself. When some of his family members finally found him, the McDonald's security officer said to them, "My, that boy can eat! He had a hamburger, three orders of fries and a coke."

THE PROPHETIC WORD OF GOD

One day I asked God where I should be paying His tithes and giving offerings. Not long after that I was passing the television set when my attention was drawn to a program sponsored by Feed the Children. In that moment, I heard God say, "Send My tithes and offerings to Larry Jones. As you open their mouths to feed them, I will open Grady's mouth to talk." And no sooner had I started blessing Feed the Children than Grady began to be more vocal. It was not yet a total conversation, but he was able to repeat back what you said to him. Now, if Grady wanted something, he would ask for it. In one way, it was a small victory, but it represented real progress.

GOD IS A GOD OF HIS WORD

With God, nothing shall be impossible. To my Christian sisters and brothers, I would say, Don't let the devil steal what rightfully belongs to you. That great man of God, Pastor C.D. McNeil, said many years ago, "Stand on the Word. If God said it, I believe it, and that settles it." Sometimes the waiting period seems for too long, but don't faint because God has promised:

> *I will never leave thee, nor forsake thee.*
>
> Hebrews 13:5

Often we ask God why a certain thing has happened to us, but we must trust that He knows all things and has a plan for our lives. It's not over until He says it's over. Place your hands in the Master's hand, and He will guide you through any storms you may encounter in life.

Chapter 3

Hearing the Voice of God

BEING IN HIS PRESENCE

The summer that Grady was about ten and a half, he went to spend the summer with his grandmother in Cleveland, and his brothers were also visiting out of the state, so our house was unusually quiet. One morning God woke me up between 4:00 and 5:00 A.M. and began talking to me in an audible voice. The power of God was very strong in my bedroom and upon me, like nothing I had experienced before or since. God was warning me about the storm I was about to go through. His precise words to me that early morning were these:

You are about to go through a storm like you have never gone through before, but in the midst of this storm I will hold you by the hand and guide you through. And, at the end of the storm, I will restore your joy and happiness!

Never in a million years could I have guessed what was about to occur!

MY STRENGTH IS IN HIS POWER

With the passage of time, Grady was growing stronger and more difficult to handle. Usually, when he had one of his rages, if he could be subdued and placed on the floor, he would quickly recover himself. It was a technique practiced by the officials in the school he was attending. I learned it from them, and then I taught the other boys how to do it without hurting him.

He loved to go to the store with his brother Cornelious, but often he would have one of his rages on the way. Cornelious finally had to stop taking him anywhere there was a crowd of people. He took him one time to his uncle's house. There Grady experienced a severe rage. Cornelius had to put him down on the ground so that he would calm down, and that particular day it was raining. When they got back from their uncle's house, they were wet and muddy. Once Cornelious had to physically pull Grady out of the car to keep him from breaking the car windows.

But, increasingly, putting Grady to the ground was not a simple thing. He was very strong, and when one of his rages had taken hold of him, his strength seemed to triple. He would wait outside a door until Cornelious came along and then attack him without warning as he came through the door. These rages continued to escalate until he was totally out of control.

WOW! ANOTHER BLESSING!

Ridge View High School opened in 1995 in Columbia, South Carolina, and Grady started school there that year. He was able to attend only two months before his rages got out of control. One day he destroyed a classroom and tried to attack anyone who attempted to stop him. A school security officer, who was 6 foot 7 and, if I recall it correctly, weighed 280 pounds, said that Grady was "just too much" for him. School officials wanted to call the police department and have Grady locked up, but, thank God, they called me first, and we were able to go rescue him yet again.

I was working now and the older boys had their jobs too, but every time Grady experienced an attack at school, one of his brothers would have to leave work and go help get him under control. This particular time, Grady was out of school for months, and I had to get assistance to have him reinstated. The school board went to great lengths to accommodate Grady's needs. One school had to rebuild some areas for his safety. Then they separated his building and room from other students and also put a lock on the door to keep him in because he was such a runner.

At that point, Grady would attack anyone who got too close to him, especially if they were trying to touch him, to calm him down. He would want to literally rip them apart. Oh, how I praise God for touching the hearts of school officials to make the accommodations needed for Grady's return to school. Wow! Another blessing!

DON'T GIVE UP ON GOD; FOR HE WON'T GIVE UP ON YOU

Each time Grady caused an incident the school would request that his doctors increase his medication. He was now on more than 759 mg of medication a day: 250 mg of Depakote, three times a day, 8 mg of Risperdal and 1 mg of Klonopin. I had never been happy about him being on medications at all because God had already told me he was going to get through this storm. Medications or not, God doesn't lie. But different schools informed me that either he would take the medications, or they would not consider accepting him. As the years progressed, different doctors tried different types of medication, but none seemed to work well enough.

I clung to God's promise for Grady and write this, even now, for his sake:

> *I will love thee, O LORD, my strength. The LORD*
> *is my rock, and my fortress, and my deliverer;*
> *my God, my strength in whom I will trust; my*
> *buckler, and the horn of my salvation, and my*
> *high tower.*   Psalm 18:1-2

Now Grady would experience rages almost every

morning before going to school, and the bus driver had to wait for him to calm down before she could get him on the bus. Any time he had to be put in the tub before going to school (because of wetting the bed), he would always fly into a rage when he was told that he had to get out. He had always loved to play in water. In time, he would have ten or more of these rages a day, triggered by various things, and I (or the other boys) always had to be on call to pick him up from school. Our lives revolved around Grady and his special needs.

In all of this, I never gave up on God because He has never given up on me. Our victory would come. We just needed to trust Him to the end.

Chapter 4

God, My Hand Is in Yours

GIVE THEM STRENGTH, GOD

One day Grady was having a very bad day at school. He attacked his teacher and ripped off her top. She placed him in a sound-proof room so he would not be able to hurt himself or others, but that didn't prevent him from hitting himself with both fists in the head over and over. At first, she was counting the blows, but she finally stopped at one hundred. She couldn't take it anymore and had to walk away. It hurt her so badly to see the child abusing himself in this way, and she felt so helpless to do anything about it. If she had tried, he would have attacked her again. She had children of her own at home, and so she couldn't take that risk. Eventually I had to go and pick Grady up that day.

On another occasion, in one of his out-of-control moments, he hit a student aide and injured her enough that she had to go to the emergency room. Praise God she recovered!

Grady's rages became so severe that the school had to hire two "body guards" to stay close to him, and they served to assist him in whatever he needed. These were big men, one of them a professional wrestler. Grady was just that strong.

GOD, YOU ARE FAITHFUL

One 4th of July a male friend and I took Grady with us to Columbia Mall. Grady asked for cookies, so we took him to the cookie shop there. While we were inside the store, Grady went into one of his rages, and it was so severe that my friend had to wrestle him to the floor so that he would calm himself.

God had to give the man the strength to do this because it was now a nearly impossible chore. The man was left with marks on his back where Grady had fought him.

When it was all over, we looked up to see that an audience of shoppers had gathered to watch what was going on. It looked to us to be over a hundred people. One lady who worked at the mall asked if we needed assistance, and a mall police officer came to help us.

It was bad enough, but it could have been much worse. We were on an upper level of the mall, and Grady, in the violent throes of his rage, could have fallen over the railing and plunged to his death. In this way, God continued to bless and help us over and over again. Our trials were not over, but God was protecting us through them.

This friend often assisted me in taking Grady out in public. He also took the two of us out for rides, out to eat or to some other place. Each time, it seemed, Grady would experience one of his rages, but God would always bring us through, because He is so faithful!

Chapter 5

In the Midst of the Storm, I Learn to Lean on God

HE IS THE WAY, THE TRUTH, AND THE LIFE

One morning I decided to take my young man out to Bojangles' for breakfast, but our outing quickly turned into a life-threatening trial. In the car, on the way to the restaurant, Grady flew into a rage and, reaching over, took hold of my hair and pulled me over to the passenger side, all the while beating on me. The miracle was that not a single car was coming in either direction because, as you can imagine, I lost control of the car.

Many years before this I was driving along one day, talking to God, and I asked Him the question: "What would I do without You?" I immediately noticed a car coming in the opposite direction heading right for me. I gripped the steering wheel firmly, closed my eyes tightly and called out the name of the Lord: "Jesus!"

I had braced myself for the impact that seemed sure to come, but now, as the seconds ticked by and I was okay, I realized that the car hadn't hit me at all. I opened my eyes and couldn't see a car anywhere in either direction. In that moment, I heard the Lord in the Spirit (very loud) say to me: "You can't do anything without Me!" Praise God that He is the way, the truth and the life (see John 14:6).

Again, God had spared me from a terrible accident, and we went on our way safely.

GOD'S LOVE IS UNCONDITIONAL

In all of this, I knew that God loved me and He loved Grady, for His love is unconditional. Jesus said:

For God so loved the world, that He gave His only begotten Son, that whosoever believeth in Him should not perish, but have everlasting life.   John 3:16

So if God loved us, why was all of this happening? Over the years, as I experienced the effects of this storm and talked to God about it, He imparted to my spirit that the storm was all about a future ministry. It was not about me or even about Grady; it was all about God's desire to help people who were hurting and discouraged by any storm. And that's just what I told anyone who was willing to listen.

One day God used an anointed prophetess to speak these very words to me: "This is not about you, but about Me." God had a great ministry that He needed to birth through us, so Grady and I were in preparation for that ministry.

Don't get me wrong. God never inflicts sickness, diseases, or infirmities upon our bodies. It is true that when Adam sinned (see Genesis 3:1-13), he brought a curse upon all mankind, but Christ has set us free from that curse:

Christ hath redeemed us from the curse of the law, being made a curse for us: for it is

written, Cursed is every one that hangeth on
a tree.   Galatians 3:13

The key is that what the devil intends for evil, God is ready to turn to our good. We see this clearly in the book of Job, where Satan obtained permission from God to tempt Job (see Job 1:6-22), and yet Satan didn't win. The Scriptures record:

> *In all this job sinned not, nor changed God fool-*
> *ishly.*   Job 1:22

Satan doesn't give up easily, but neither should we, as sons of God. We must fight a good fight, keeping on the breastplate of faith.

WAIT ON THE LORD

Then the devil obtained permission to tempt Job further (see Job 2:1-8), and the result was that Job lost everything he'd had: his houses, his animals and even his children. His wife thought he should just curse God and die, but he refused:

> *But he said unto her, Thou speakest as one of*
> *the foolish women speaketh. What? Shall we*

receive good at the hand of God, and shall we not receive evil? In all this did not Job sin with his lips. Job 2:10

The result was that God blessed Job even more than before:

The LORD gave Job twice as much as he had before. Job 42:10

So the LORD blessed the latter end of Job more than his beginning. Job 42:12

To you, dear reader, I say, whatever you are going through, WAIT ON THE LORD! His promise is this:

But they that wait upon the LORD shall renew their strength; they shall mount up with wings as eagles; they shall run, and not be weary; and they shall walk and not faint. Isaiah 40:31

Your day of victory is coming too!

Chapter 6

The Just Shall Live by Faith

FAITHFUL IS HIS NAME

One night I received a call about 1:00 A.M. "Is this Ms. Lee?" a lady asked.

"It is," I answered, wondering where this conversation might be going.

"I'm a friend of Cornelious," the lady continued. She said she was calling from a nearby store.

My heart leaped. Some years before I had gotten

the news in the early hours of the morning that Cornelious had been in a serious auto accident. The Lord had been gracious to him on that occasion. Had he been in another accident perhaps?

But now the conversation turned. "Where's Grady?" the lady asked.

I thought it was very unusual for her to ask about Grady, but I answered her nevertheless: "He's in bed."

"You'll be surprised to know that he's standing right here in front of me, and he has in his hand one of the biggest Hershey bars," she said.

I was shocked. When I had gone to bed, Grady had been in his bed asleep, but apparently he had awakened, gotten out of bed and gone to the corner store, wanting to get a candy bar. Of course he had no money.

Thank God, this lady had been kind enough to call me.

Grady was still in his pajamas (thankfully he had put on his flip flops), and why he didn't remember that we had plenty of snacks at home I'll never know, but this was my surprise of the night.

God had protected my son on his walk to the store, and now the kind lady who had called to report his whereabouts brought him back to the house. She also paid for his Hershey bar, but I couldn't let him eat it because he hadn't paid for it. These were simple lessons that he needed to learn. From that time on, I had to be more alert at night, and I had to check on Grady more often. PRAISE GOD! FAITHFUL IS HIS NAME!

JEHOVAH, MY PEACE (SHALOM)

At one point Grady got out of control again and had to be put in Baptist Hospital for a whole month to adjust his medications. It touches any mother's heart to leave her child when that child is crying to go with her, and Grady had to be hospitalized many times through the years. I was always there for him, or one of his brothers was, and eventually he realized that if we had to leave for a while, we would be coming back, so he relaxed about it. In this way, God gave us all peace.

GOD'S STILL IN CHARGE

It was a happy day for us all when Grady was discharged from the hospital and could come home again. His grandmother brought him a big teddy bear. He decided to throw it out the car window, and I had to leave it on the highway, but he was very glad to be back at home, and we were all glad to have him back where he belonged.

One day I received a phone call from a social agency asking if I would like to place my son in a group home. Because of Grady's frequent rages, school officials had suggested that this agency call us. They felt we needed help. In the particular group home they had in mind, they already had three autistic young men, and they had room for one more.

"Grady has a home," I told them. I wasn't about to put my son in such a home. Adolphus agreed. He had told me years before that he and his brother were willing to help out with Grady so that he would never be forced to move to such a home. And, praise God, they had been faithful to that commitment. What a blessing my two older sons have been!

JEHOVAH (GOD) WILL COMFORT YOU

When Grady came home from the hospital, I had to work the next day, so I got up early and went to the store to pick up a few items to fix breakfast for Grady and Adolphus, who were both still sleeping. When I got back, I found Adolphus still in bed, but Grady was nowhere to be found. I called a friend to come and help us look for him. Adolphus searched on foot, and my friend and I searched by car. After an hour of searching, we still couldn't locate Grady. I really didn't want to call 911, but, at that point, it seemed that I had no choice. Mama's Boy was nowhere in sight.

When I called 911, I was told that no calls had come in about anyone fitting my son's description, but no sooner had I hung up than they called back. Grady had been picked up by a police officer and was, at that moment, in the back seat of his squad car. Sure enough, he was still in his pajamas and flip flops. He was now on a different medication, so we had hoped that his wandering would be a thing of the past, but apparently it was not so.

Soon my friend spotted the police car with Grady in the back seat. It was heading in the opposite direction toward police headquarters. Trying not to drive too fast, so as to avoid getting a ticket, my friend flagged the police car down.

Grady was perfectly content, sitting in the back seat, eating onion rings. "Look, everybody," he said. "I'm not wearing handcuffs!" God was blessing us over and over again.

The police officer was asked to take Grady on home in the squad car, and he agreed. The story was that Grady had been spotted crossing the road near where I worked. As the officer approached, he heard the squealing sound as a car slammed on its brakes and swerved to avoid hitting Grady. When Grady wanted to cross a road, he didn't yield to anyone, but, again, God had been on his side, and he was spared serious injury or death.

Apparently Grady had been missing me so much during his stay in the hospital that he decided to take it upon himself to go see me at my work. What great love!

The policeman suggested to our landlord that he put dead bolts on the doors, the kind that only opened from the inside with a key. As it turned out, it was against the law to have those kinds of dead bolts, because they were considered dangerous during an emergency, such as a fire. But I was now given permission to install them. I found that I could never leave the key in them because Grady was always watching out of the corner of his eye to see if I forgot to take the key out. He always seemed to be looking for his next move, but thankfully, God was always ready to protect him. And He was also always ready to comfort me as a mother in whatever we happened to be going through at the moment.

Chapter 7

Experiencing the Angels of the Lord

HIS POWER DOESN'T DECREASE; RATHER, IT INCREASES

One morning, as I was dressing and applying my makeup for work, Grady was in the kitchen, eating breakfast and waiting for the school bus. The next thing I knew he was in the bathroom in a very high rage. When I went in to help him, he pushed me to the floor, and we struggled.

Grady wouldn't stop hitting me, so I picked up the clothes hamper and put it on top of me to ward off his blows. He stood there for a while trying to figure out how he could get to me, and then, in his anger, he started hitting himself with his fists.

Finally, he calmed down, and I was able to clean his face and hair again and then put him on the school bus. I was a mess and would have to redo my makeup, and the bathroom looked like someone had broken into it. There were curlers strewn everywhere and lots of other things out of their place. Besides two bloody knees and a ten-to-fifteen-minute job of beautifying myself again for work, I had peace. Praise God!

Grady had always kept himself very busy. If there was nothing else exciting to do, he would walk back and forth and back and forth all day long. He didn't enjoy watching television, but eating and playing in water were his two favorite things. I had always known that he was precious to God, because he was so precious to me, and I was determined to withstand this storm through God's strength working in me. Glory to His name! His power really doesn't decrease; rather, it increases!

A CALL TO PRAISE GOD

For he shall give his angels change over thee, to keep thee in all thy ways.   Psalm 91:11

One night Grady began experiencing a very severe rage. I was tired—worn out, in fact—and I needed to rest, but not Grady. He jumped up and down in his bed, biting his fingers, hitting himself in the head and making loud noises.

This had been going on now for so many weeks and months that I cried unto the Lord that night for His help. I was led to call on Michael, the archangel, to come to my rescue. I said, "I command you, Michael, the archangel, to come forth and place your hands on Grady to calm him." It was my first time to call on Michael for help (although I had called upon other angels) and, of course, always called on the name of the Lord.

I was standing at the foot of Grady's bed and was able to witness the fact that he felt someone or something touch him. He had been in the process of lying down and putting his face toward the wall, but now he turned and looked at my hands. He seemed surprised to see them at my side. Then who had touched him?

Next he looked toward the floor, saw Michael's feet, and was terrified. "Oh! Oh! Oh!" he gasped.

His eyes followed Michael from the floor to the ceiling, and again he uttered those words of fear, "Oh! Oh! Oh!"

I watched Grady as he looked the angel over from head to foot. Michael, the archangel, was there by his bedside, ready to do battle against every evil spirit that was attacking my son. I could not see him myself, but Grady's observation of him was clear. Within seconds, his fear turned to peace, joy and a great big smile.

I continued to watch Grady for a while, interacting with the angel Michael! I can never forget that night.

For many months afterward, when I got Grady up during the night to use the bathroom, he would go back to bed and pull his pillow over his head. Then he would cover that with his blanket. When I asked him why he was doing that, he said because of Michael. I noticed every night that he would look directly at the spot where Michael, the archangel, had stood. He must have been saying that it was great to have Michael's protection but not every night perhaps. Oh, the power of our Lord Jesus Christ!

GOD'S EVERLASTING PROTECTION

The angelic visitations didn't stop there. One day I walked into Grady's bedroom and again found him in the presence of an angel. I hurried into the next room to get Cornelious, and together we stood and watched Grady interact with his angel. Grady kept closing and then opening his eyes. He would smile with a very pleasant look. And you could feel the presence of peace in that room. God was continuing to bless us in this very special way.

Chapter 8

The Everlasting Presence and Power of God

GOD'S SUSTAINING POWER

I will lift up mine eyes unto the hills from whence cometh my help. My help cometh from the LORD, which made heaven and earth.

Psalm 121:1-2

At one point, Grady had a caregiver, Mrs. Terry Taylor, who would keep him after school until his older brother could pick him up and bring him home. It wasn't unusual for Grady to go into a rage in the car on the way home.

One particular day, his caregiver decided to take him out with her. She stopped to get some gasoline in her car, but while she was pumping the gas, Grady jumped out of the car and went into the store. She ran into the store behind him, but then, as she was going in one door, he was darting out another.

When he took off running down a main highway toward the Interstate, she was unable to follow him because of health problems, so she called me to let me know what had happened. She was sorry, but because of what she was going through at the time, there was nothing she could do.

But our God is the all-knowing God, and He had everything already planned for this particular situation and time. When the caregiver called, I was at home. Adolphus had stopped by and had just left to go to his home, and Cornelious had just walked in. I called Adolphus and asked where he was. He was ten minutes away from Grady. I asked him to go help his brother and said that I was on my way too and I told Cornelious the same thing. Then, I called on Michael the archangel again, in the name of the Lord. I gave Michael very specific commands:

to go to Farrow Road, in Columbia, South Carolina, to help Grady D. Lee.

I prayed as I was changing clothes. I knew it was time for war, and I intended to have on my full battle armor:

> *Then he said, "Don't be afraid, Daniel. Since the first day you began to pray for understanding and to humble yourself before your God, your request has been heard in heaven. I have come in answer to your prayer. But for twenty-one days the spirit prince of the kingdom of Persia blocked my way. Then Michael, one of the archangels, came to help me, and I left him there with the spirit prince of the kingdom of Persia."*
>
> Daniel 10:12-13, NLT

When I got in the car, I noticed that my gas gauge was on empty. My mother had always said to me, "Make sure you keep gas in the car in case of an emergency," but I hadn't taken her good advice this time. Now it was time for a double prayer. I said, "God, I have the money to purchase the gas, but I don't have the time to stop for it. I need You now as never before!" His Word had promised:

Be careful for nothing; but in everything by prayer and supplication with thanksgiving let your requests be made known unto God.

Philippians 4:6

In that moment, I watched the hand of God perform a miracle. With my own eyes I saw the needle on the gas gauge start to move up. What an awesome God we serve!

I love talking to my Daddy (God), and that day I said to Him, "God, You could have put it on full!" I laughed. Thank God He has a sense of humor and knows the heart of every man. He gave me enough gas to get to where I was going and back home with a little left over. He is a God of more than enough.

HE IS A RIGHT-NOW GOD

When I arrived at the store, I didn't see anyone but Adolphus. He told me that Cornelious had Grady, and they were at Mrs. Terry's house. When I arrived there, Grady was sitting down, looking as if he was the quietest child on the block. Mrs. Terry informed me that Grady had been running so fast that his pants were falling down. He had run in front of cars at the main intersection of Farrow and Hardscrabble

Roads. But God had every car to stop or slow down for Grady.

Cornelious said he saw two men get out a white truck to help Grady, but he pulled away from them and kept on running. I believe these were not just regular men, but angels, who obey the commands of the Word of God. We are the sons of God, and, as such, we have the authority to command our angels to protect us. Michael, the archangel, had definitely been on the scene that day. Just one touch means so much.

Mrs. Terry said she had gotten in her car to go pick Grady up, and when she reached him, he was totally calm and willingly got into the car. Thank God! Trust in Him, and He will fight every battle for you. He is a right-now God!

Chapter 9

They that Sow in Tears Shall Reap in Joy

THE JOY OF THE LORD IS MY STRENGTH

I cried unto the LORD with my voice; with my voice unto the LORD did I make my supplication. Psalm 142:1

So many times I would look at my beloved son being tormented with those uncontrollable rages, and I was tempted to despair of ever finding help for him. But I never doubted God and always knew that God would bring Him out. Glory to His name!

I have shed many tears for Grady, but none of them were tears of sorrow. Rather, they were tears of joy, as I kept in my mind God's vision for my son. I was believing that God would bring him out of this situation. At the moment, all I could do was call out to the Lord, for He was the only solution, and my answer would come through prayer, faith in God, the Word of God and praise.

What a beautiful combination! Prayer changes things, faith moves God, and His Word works. Sometimes after being abused by Grady, I shed tears before the Lord, but then I vowed before Him: "Lord, I will get through this storm. In the meantime, just hold me by my hand, and I won't let go until You have accomplished a good work in me. When I am tried, I will come forth as pure gold. You are my strength."

I WILL PRAISE HIM
WITH MY WHOLE HEART

And thou shalt love the LORD thy God with all thine heart, and with all thy soul, and with all thy might.   Deuteronomy 6:5

This is the first and great commandment.

Matthew 22:38

I loved God so much that I wanted to be obedient to His commandments and not fail Him in any way. When you truly fall deeply in love with your whole heart, you lose yourself in the process. I was determined for God's will to be done in my life, so I determined to fight every demonic force that was hindering my son and keeping him from his complete deliverance.

Over the years, God had entrusted to me a deliverance ministry, and so, with the power and authority He had given me, I was determined to win this war. Always remember, the battle is not yours, but God's. He said:

> *For we wrestle not against flesh and blood, but against principalities, against powers, against the rulers of the darkness of this world, against spiritual wickedness in high places.*
>
> Ephesians 6:12

I preached a sermon from Daniel 3:1-30 entitled "The Word, Faith and Praise in the Fiery Furnace." Like those Hebrew boys, sometimes your furnace will be turned up seven times hotter. But through everything, you will find the Fourth Man showing up (the Lord). Hold on to His hand, and He won't let you go!

At times I felt like I had been through World Wars I, II, and Vietnam combined, but guess what? I was back, and I was stronger than ever, with power and strength through my Lord and Savior Jesus Christ!

> *Nay, in all these things we are more than conquerors through him that loved us.*
>
> Romans 8:37

FOR WITH GOD NOTHING SHALL BE IMPOSSIBLE

Now Grady had to be hospitalized in a mental Institution. His rages were getting worse. I received a call that he'd had to be moved to another building. Because the majority of the employees in the hospital were women, they had transferred him to a section overseen by men, because they were stronger and better able to deal with him.

Later, I learned that juveniles from a nearby prison had been sent to the same facility for evaluation. My precious son was now locked up with rapists and murders. When I complained about this, Grady was quickly discharged. One of the employees at the hospital later told me, "Grady can hold his own. Those other inmates would back up with fear when Grady walked through." His rages were too severe even for these hardened men to handle.

What would happen to us now? I knew that what the devil had set for evil, God had worked out for Grady's good. With God, nothing shall be impossible. Nothing!

Chapter 10

God Is My Solid Rock

STAND FIRM ON HIS FOUNDATION

Therefore whosoever heareth these sayings of mine, and doeth them, I will liken unto a wise man, which built his house upon a rock.

Matthew 7:24

Through my storm, I never, not even once, thought that God had forsaken me. With God as my Father and Jesus as my Brother, I couldn't lose with the power They use! I learned to lean on them, because they are a strong foundation. Thank God, Satan lost his power:

> *And Jesus came and spake unto them, saying, All power is given unto me in heaven and in earth.*   Matthew 28:18

Praise God! How good it is to be on the Lord's side. Jesus said:

> *Behold, I give unto you power to tread on serpents and scorpions, and over all the power of the enemy: and nothing shall by any means hurt you.*   Luke 10:19

I had to know who I was in Christ Jesus.

Grady would often get up in the middle of the night and, because of this, I lost years of sleep. Sometimes he would wake up between 3:00 and 4:00 A.M. and experience a high rage. One night I sensed someone standing over my bed, and when I opened my eyes I could see that it was Grady. He had been watching me in the half-darken room, and I could see by his facial expression that he was about to go into a rage.

I moved to the right side of the bed, and he moved that way to attack me. I moved to the left side, and he ran to that side. I had to think quickly how I could get out of this situation. Grady was now a man, and I had learned a long time ago not to let him get me lying on my back, or I couldn't get away from him.

I lay very still for a moment and watched to see what his next move would be. He decided to climb in the bed from the foot, but I had sensed that this was what he would do and had said to myself, "When he does, roll to the left and get out of the room as quickly as possible."

It worked. Eventually Grady calmed down and went back to bed, and my foundation was still strong and solid in Christ.

GOD IS OUR PRESENT HELP IN TIME OF TROUBLE

One night Grady got up and decided to make some peanut butter and jelly sandwiches. He used an entire loaf of bread and had jelly all over the counter and the floor. When I heard someone in the kitchen, I knew that it was him. I certainly didn't have a maid, although I needed one that night to clean up Grady's mess.

After he had eaten his peanut butter and jelly sandwiches, he was fine, but he wasn't sleepy. And so another night of sleep was lost.

He did this so many times that eventually I had to buy a chain and lock to put on the refrigerator door. Thank God that resolved the problem.

One day when Grady was still a teenager and his brothers were still living at home, he went into a rage and caught Cornelious off guard, lying on the couch. He kicked Cornelious into the wall. He hit the wall so hard that his buttock went through the wall board and left a big hole. I was at work when this occurred, and from then on, I was never quite sure what might happen.

One day when Grady and I were about to go out, he fell into a rage at the door. He turned and ran into the bedroom and began jumping up and down on the bed with his shoes on. I stood close to the bed, trying to calm him down. Before I knew it, he had jumped very high and, on his way down, kicked me in my chest with his feet. His thrust was so powerful that it sent me flying across the room in the air. I landed on my rear, and the back of my head hit the closet door. I was stunned and had to shake myself for a while to get myself together.

When I looked up, Grady was coming for round two. I jumped up quickly to avoid his wrath and help him calm down. After he had calmed down, everything was fine. When trouble is present, trust God, and He will be your help!

WE STILL HAVE VICTORY

Whenever we were riding in the car, Grady would try to get out. If he had gone into a rage in the back seat, he would try to climb over into the front to attack me. We had learned to put the safety lock on the back door, but then he would climb over the front seats to get out the front door.

Cornelious would take him for a ride, but when they walked back in the door, I could tell they had just come from a war zone. Ironically, Grady always enjoyed going for a ride, but his rages were becoming more and more severe. Sometimes we couldn't make it to the stop sign at the corner of the first block before he erupted. This led to his having to be confined to the house. Because of this, my life and the lives of my other sons had to totally change, but we still had the victory.

GOD'S PROTECTION WITH THE CAREGIVERS

Grady had wonderful caregivers, and I thank God

for each one of them. He had a sitter who loved him so much that she kept him one summer. Grady picked up twenty pounds in those few months. She would cut up fresh potatoes every morning to cook him French fries for breakfast. It was one of his favorite foods.

What an awesome woman! I'm his mother, and I didn't cook him fresh fries. I did sometimes buy the frozen fries or the fries from McDonald's or Bojangles'. But she took very good care of him! In the regular times, each morning she would come to the car and get him out. That saved me so much time and helped me get to work. Then one day, in a rage, Grady hit her daughter. That frightened her. The girls was so much younger and smaller than Grady. In the end, she decided that she couldn't keep Grady anymore.

Grady had another lady caregiver who worked just two days a week. By the second day she said the rages were becoming too much for her. I understood completely. My sister Linda Caughman assisted with Grady, giving me and my sons a much-needed break sometimes. Grady would have great rages around her. Fortunately sometimes her sons were there, to assist with him and help to calm him down.

I was working on my job one Friday, and I had to

take Grady with me. I said, "Lord, I can't have him up here for hours until his brother are able to pick him up," and I started praying for the Lord to intervene. Within about thirty minutes, my sister walked in the door and offered to take him with her. Don't tell me that God is not a right-now God!

Then, as time passed, Grady had a severe rage one day at my sister's house too. Her son was there to calm him down, but she later told me that she was frightened of him and couldn't keep him anymore. God's power was always there to protect! I understood completely.

WHAT DO YOU DO WHEN YOU DON'T KNOW WHAT TO DO?

Sometimes things could become very intense for anyone caring for Grady. Cornelious picked him up from Mrs. Terry's house one day and decided to stop at the sub station on Park Lane, but he was not thinking very clearly. Grady lost no time in getting out of the car and started running down a very busy street and onto Park Lane. He was running toward Columbia Mall on a Friday evening.

Cornelious had on steel boots that kept him from

running well, and this time Grady, who seemed to be running the Olympics, won the race, reaching the mall before his brother could overtake and stop him. But even then, he didn't stop running. He kept running headlong right through the mall.

As he ran through the mall at breakneck speed, I'm sure people who saw him that day must have been wondering if he had just committed some crime and was trying to escape.

To his credit, Cornelious didn't give up. He was some distance behind his younger brother, but he kept running with all of his might to catch him. Eventually a mall officer saw what was happening and tried to intervene.

Cornelious was desperate to stop his brother before he ran into some store. If he did that, he might never find him. Also he knew how very violent Grady could be if he felt threatened. At one point, he had kicked a ten-month old child in the face. Fortunately, she was not seriously injured. But this was a frightening experience for Cornelious. But God had a plan in motion.

Cornelious called to inform me of what had happened. He said, "Mama, I had to leave my keys in the car and let it sit there because Grady came first." That was very meaningful. Cornelious had just recently purchased a new expensive ride. Praise God the angels were not only with Grady, but also with Cornelious' vehicle, and no harm came to it.

When I went to the mall to pick them up, Cornelious was still out of breathe and coughing, but Grady was standing there, full of energy, like he was ready to go another round. We went by to pick up Cornelious' car at the restaurant.

The heart of the security officer at the mall had gone out to us as he walked us to the car. He said, "Woman, may God bless you."

What a great son Cornelious has been! Another day had passed with the safety of the Lord in evidence over our lives. When you don't know what to do, trust God!

Chapter 11

Lord, I Need a Touch from You

NO ONE ELSE CAN DO THE THINGS YOU DO

Grady's rages continued to increase in intensity, and since he was becoming stronger all the time, it presented a more dangerous situation every day. No one but Almighty God Himself kept me in perfect peace through it all. Now close relatives pleaded with me to put him into an institution. "If you don't," they warned, "he's going to hurt you bad."

Not surprisingly, I received the same advice from school officials and doctors, but my response was always the same: "God said He would bring Grady through this. So whose report will you believe? I believe the report of the Lord."

The last time Grady was institutionalized (hospitalized) and placed behind locked doors (because of the other inmates), I promise him that I would make sure he had the help of a prominent doctor. I prayed about that, and God opened the door for him to see a very wonderful doctor at Baptist Hospital in Columbia.

Prayer changes things, and God blessed Grady with Doctor Timothy D. Malone. We could see quickly that he was a very kind, meek and wonderful man, with a caring heart. May God bless him and his assistant, Bobbie, in the name of Jesus.

Eventually Dr. Malone increased Grady's medication until he was now taking 1,000 mg of Depakote, 500 mg of Seroquel, 4 mg of Risperdal, .3 mg of Cloridine, and 900 mg of Lithium every day. That was 2,404.3 mg of medicine a day, and still the rages continued. God had showed me that the storm had to come, no matter how much medication Grady was on, and I know that God could not lie. The Bible shows that a lie is an impossibility for Him (see Hebrews 6:18).

As noted earlier, I was still not happy about Grady being on so much medication, but the schools he was attending would not permit him to continue without it, and I had to work at the time, to keep our family going, so all I could do was keep my peace and maintain my faith in God. While we're trying to figure things out, God already has it all worked out. God, no one else can do the things You do!

THE BATTLE IS NOT YOURS BUT THE LORD'S

As Grady began taking this increase in medication, his body started to change. He would use the bathroom frequently, and he was thirsty continually. Sometimes, at night, he would need to use the bathroom four or five times, and I wasn't always able to wake him up, so he wet his bed most every night.

Each morning, while getting ready for work, I would start washing Grady's dirty laundry. I could never finish it before work, for it was too many loads to wash in two hours. I would have to finish when

I got back home from work in the afternoon. This went on for many months.

In this way, I worked before I went to work. But, I did what I had to do without complaining, and I did it unto the Lord.

Grady was very angry one day. He was standing by a very large brass and glass divider, and that was not a very safe place for him to be standing when he got upset. Something in me said, "Don't even look at it, to give him the idea." But it seemed like Grady was reading my mind. He looked at me and then turned his gaze toward the glass divider, back at me and then back to the divider. I saw what was about to happen and was saying to myself, "Oh, no!" But, oh, yes, he pushed it over on the floor, and in the process broke many valuable items that could not be replaced.

I was praising God that he hadn't pushed it over on himself or on me. Adolphus was home to help me with the mess and with Grady. Our battle belongs to the Lord!

BECAUSE HE LIVES
I CAN FACE TOMORROW

That was not the end of the things Grady destroyed. He continued to destroy things. He threw a television set that I had placed in his room into the wall and broke it. Needless to say, I didn't buy him another one. There were many things that I and my other sons could not buy or have around during those years simply because they would have been destroyed during one of Grady's rages.

He was very destructive. He would jump up and down uncontrollably on the den couch and also on his bed. It was a terrible habit that we could not seem to break, and during one period of rage, he broke the base of the den couch and destroyed his own mattress and box springs.

Cornelious and I would clean all day and half of the night, and then Grady would be eating at the table and, before you knew it, he was running through the house in a rage with food in his hand, throwing it everywhere—on the walls, the floors and the furniture.

Grady had always enjoyed eating, but his appetite ballooned when he was on certain medications. When he was fifteen he weighed 124 pounds, but then, because of the addition of a new medication, he gained 100 pounds and became 46 inches in the waist. Mama's Little Man had suddenly become Mama's Sweet Big Man.

Although Grady had gained a great amount of weight, he looked handsome to me. Eventually, he lost that weight when he was taken off of the medicine.

On many nights we gave Grady food to take to bed just so that we could get some rest. He would lie in his bed and snack until he fell asleep. The next morning, when Adolphus would come over to help out, he had to pull the bed out and vacuum all around it, and he wasn't happy about that. But Mama had to do what Mama had to do to get enough rest. Praise God for snacks!

STANDING IN THE NEED OF PRAYER

God began to speak to me in dreams and visions. In one dream, I was driving a car, and the brakes failed. I was going over a bridge, and I lamented, "I can't swim!" Then my faith began to activate, and I started believing that I would survive this ordeal too. I looked up and saw three angels, as bright as the sun. A bright glow shined all around them. My eyes couldn't totally take them in, but I was able to see their white garments.

My faith was activated first, and then my angels came on the scene, and the result was that my car started floating on top of the water. Faith moves God and changes your situation. The bridge represented something that holds you up in times of difficulty. The water represented the move of the Holy Spirit. The angels were my protection. God was letting me know that during my difficult moments in the storm He would protect me with His power and hold me up, so that I would not drown, but survive. I knew that He would be there for me. It's so good to know our God!

BE PATIENT WITH GOD; HE IS NOT THROUGH WITH YOU YET

I gave birth to two sons I have not yet mentioned. One of them was born on November 29, 1985. I named him Paul because he had suffered for eight months in my womb, as the disciple Paul of the Bible suffered greatly in life. God used the biblical Paul to help turn this world into a better place, so I considered it to be a worthy name on two counts.

In the 29th week of my pregnancy, I was diagnosed with complications known as non-immune hydrops or hydrops fetalis. This is a very serious condition, and the prognosis for the unborn fetus is usually very poor. The condition can also threaten the health and well-being of the mother. During my pregnancy, I was hospitalized on quite a few occasions at Wilford Hall Medical Center at Lackland Air Force Base in Texas. While I was there, I missed my family very much, especially Grady. He suffered too, being apart from Mama, but at least he had his Daddy and his older brothers. When he'd had to be hospitalized, he was alone, totally separated from family, and that was very hard for all of us.

I was treated there in Texas because my husband was in the Army, stationed at Killeen. This hospital, three hours away from there, specialize in the type of severe illnesses I and my unborn child were suffering. On several of these occasions, I had to be hospitalized for weeks at a time.

Doctors advised me, early on, of the seriousness of the illness and that Paul would probably not live long after birth. That was hard to hear. He was already a part of me, and I loved him very much. But his lungs, I was told, were severely impaired, and he would have difficulty breathing on his own.

A great woman of God told me that God was waiting for my decision. Was I ready and willing to care for another mentally-challenged child? Or would I release this son to God? What a difficult decision it was! I surely couldn't make such a decision quickly or without talking long and hard with God about it. In the end, with many tears and prayers, I released Paul to my heavenly Father on November 27, 1985. The very next day I went into labor.

I was home at the time, and I asked my husband to please not take me to the hospital just yet. I was only having light pain (it was my fifth pregnancy, so I knew the difference), and I wanted Paul to be able to spend one more day with the family. Besides, it was Thanksgiving Day.

The next day, November 29, 1985, my husband took me to Fort Hood Army Hospital in Killeen. When I arrived, a doctor confirmed that I was in labor, and, before long, determined that the child was in danger. His heart rate was dropping. A priest was called for, and he came in to pray with me. When I saw him walking through the door, I sensed that Paul would soon be with God.

I was content with my decision. What better place for my son to be than in the loving arms of the heavenly Father? There he would be totally healed. Praise God!

ANOTHER TRIP,
WITH GOD ON MY SIDE

Because of the danger to my own health, the doctor at Lackland decided to send me back to Wilford Hall Medical Center in an ambulance. My family drove down to be with me.

When I arrived at the hospital, the doctors and their staffs—my physician and his staff and Paul's physician and her staff—were waiting for me in the delivery room. Some fifteen well-trained professionals were in position ready to do what they could to save my life and to make Paul as comfortable as possible. I had released him to God, but I didn't feel that God wanted me to die too. My family needed me.

Before long I gave birth to a seven-pound baby boy whom we had already named Paul Lee. Two hours later, Paul went into cardiopulmonary arrest from lung complications and died. I didn't get a chance to see this son alive because he had been delivered by C-section, and I was still in the recovery room under the effects of the anesthesia. By the time I came around, he was already in the bosom of our Father God.

At our request, the staff brought Paul's lifeless

body into my room so that our family could spend an hour with him. I thank God for such a wonderful staff.

Adolphus, who was just six at the time, when he saw Paul in my arms, said, "Mama, you said Paul was dead." I had to explain to him that Paul's body was there for the funeral and burial, but that his soul and spirit were already with God. The Word of God tells us:

> *We are confident, I say, and willing rather to be absent from the body, and to be present with the Lord.* 2 Corinthians 5:8

Paul was buried on December 5, 1985, but a loving mother can never forget her child. I will be looking forward to see all of my precious sons the day I make it to my Father's House.

I have yet another son who is in the bosom of God. He was my second oldest, but he was stillborn. He never got the chance to look into his mother's eyes, but one day he will see my beautiful smile. I carried him eight and a half months, and he was already more than eight pounds.

The reason I have told Paul's story here is because he played a special role in Grady's life. One night, when I was mentally and physical exhausted from caring for Grady, Paul appeared to me in a dream. I couldn't see him very clearly, but what he said to me was very clear: "Hi, Mom! This is your son Paul. Don't give up on Grady."

It was just what I needed to hear at that moment. God gave me renewed strength through Paul's words, and I awoke refreshed, and feeling strengthened and ready to continue the battle. Be patient with God; He is on your side!

Chapter 12

I Never Would Have Made It without You

HE IS ABLE TO BRING YOU OUT

Grady was getting close to being able to graduate from Spring Valley High School here in Columbia, South Carolina. With all of his trials, he had successfully remained in school since he was just three and a half years old, and he was now twenty-one.

What a blessing a graduation would be! It had been such a struggle trying to keep him in school because of his uncontrollable rages. But, glory to God, with His power and strength, Grady had made it. Hallelujah!

Then, just two weeks before his scheduled graduation, Grady attacked his bus driver. While the bus was moving along, he got up out of his seat, went forward and started hitting her from behind. She was injured enough that she had to be hospitalized. Thank God she didn't have an accident, and thank God she recovered. This was Grady's final severe school rage.

School officials were gracious to Grady, and on May 13, 2003, he graduated from high school. God had been faithful to him for seventeen and a half years.

By this time, God had already told me to quit my job because, He said, He was preparing me for war. It happened one day as I was on my way to McDonald's for a cup of coffee. I had passed my work place and looked to see if anyone was waiting for me to open the store. I really didn't feel like going to work that day because I had so many things to do at there.

I had my car radio on, and I was enjoying some good Christian music, when the Lord spoke to me and said, "It's time to come off your job and walk totally in faith." For a second, I forgot that I was driving. I closed my eyes, and, with both hands, slapped my cheeks. I said very loudly, "God, that's a lot of faith!" The image of my unpaid bills were rolling before my eyes, and the car I was driving was not yet paid for.

I heard a car pass, and was drawn back to the realization that I was out driving. I gripped the steeling wheel and marveled that my angels had taken charge of the car while I had been pondering God's words.

As I entered the workplace that day, I said to God, "Yes! I'm willing. Just let me know when."

LET GO AND LET GOD

Several days later, God gave me a dream about coming off of my job. I was standing in the back of the store in the stock room, and the ceiling suddenly opened up, and water started pouring in. I felt the presence of someone very huge and nearly as tall as the ceiling behind me. I didn't turn around to see who it was.

God then gave me the interpretation of the dream. The huge, tall person was my guardian angel, always there to protect me in every storm. I said to him, "Let me go into the other room to lock the doors because a storm is coming." When I entered the other room what I saw was a hurricane, a very turbulent storm. The store was now completely empty; it contained not a single item or fixture.

I believe this all happened on a Thursday. That Sunday I went out of town to visit my parents' church, and there I received a prophetic word from an anointed prophetess. Through her, God said, "It is now time to come off your job." He apparently wasn't giving me even time to save up money to pay my bills. I would soon be walking by faith in Him.

I said, "Yes, God, I will." In all of this, God was letting me know of the severity of the storm I would now face with Grady, and the interpretation of the dream was that my storm had already started. When I was in that back room and the ceiling had opened, it meant that the storm would pour down upon me severely. But God was also saying, "Your angel will protect you, but come out now for you are in the middle of the storm."

When we have a hurricane and the weatherman watches the eye of the storm, it is because what is happening in the eye of the storm is a predictor of how severe the storm will be. God told me He would hold me by my hand in the middle of this storm. It would be fierce.

Being in the middle of a storm can take you under if God is not there to help you. After prayer, I decided to give my employer a three-week notice of my resignation. I can still remember the day I finally walked out that door for the last time. Everyone there was sure I would change my mind about quitting before that day came, but when I walked out, it was with a very big smile on my face.

I really didn't know what was ahead of me. I was about to face a great storm with no source of income and only my faith in God to sustain me. My new journey had just begun. I had let go and let God!

I NEED YOU NOW, LORD!

It didn't take me long to realize I was in the dead middle of the storm. God had called it a turbulent storm, and I soon felt its effects. The *New Oxford American Dictionary* defines *turbulent* this way: "characterized by conflict, disorder, or confusion; not controlled or calm, moving unsteadily or violently." I understood very well that I could not have worked and gone through such a turbulent storm. It was now just too much for me to try to focus on Grady and work at the same time.

I felt sure that if I chose not to obey God and, instead, to continue to work, I would have become ill, mentally and physically. I thank God that I was obedient to Him. He said that to obey is better than sacrifice.

Now Grady's rages went to a new level, so that I cried out to God, "My God! My God! I need You now as never before!" I was exhausted from his frequent and violent rages, and he was sleeping less than ever, and making it difficult for me to sleep as well.

I was led to start playing the Bible on cassette tape for him while he was bathing. He still loved to play in the water, and so a bubble bath was great fun for him. It also seemed like the perfect time for him to listen to God's Word. The bath kept him calm long enough to get some of the Word of God into his spirit.

Later, I started playing CD's with anointed music and what was being called throne room songs. People who were experiencing God's glory were singing, and it almost sounded like the angels. This placed Grady in the glory of God.

I had been learning that anointed music can break yokes, and I could sense that it was working with Grady. I realized that God had not called me to leave my work to sit and cry. It was so that I could begin to birth Grady into his ministry and calling through the power of His glory. I had to do it through faith because the enemy was fighting it tooth and nail. But even as the enemy waged his desperate attacks, God was calling me to stand on the Word and work the Word, through faith.

One day Jesus healed ten lepers, and only one of them returned to give Him glory. Jesus said to him that day:

> *Arise, go thy way: thy faith hath made thee whole.*   Luke 17:19

Not only had this man been healed, but now, because he had returned to give glory to God, he was made whole. This means that any body parts that were missing were restored. And God hasn't changed. He want us to have faith in Him, to trust Him in everything.

Believing God results in great blessing—spiritually, financially and physically—blessings for every aspect of our lives. And God wants to bless us today just as He healed those lepers. For He is the same God yesterday, today and forevermore. Yes, our faith moves God!

EVERY PROMISE IS MINE

I resigned from my job on June 8, 2000, and so this coming June will mark ten years of trusting God for all my needs. He is my Jehovah Jireh, my Provider, and He has really taken good care of me. I have been blessed even more financial since I left my secular job and began to walk in obedience to Him.

Grady has an uncle and aunt who have been a great blessing to us. Uncle Willie and Aunt Louise Brown bless us with bags of meat that sometimes last for a full month. Praise God! That saves so much on our grocery bill. God has been using them over and over again in this way now for going on ten years.

Uncle Willie loves to send us the best meats: ribs, hams, pork chops, fish, chicken, steak and more. And he always gives us the family packs. God's Word is true when it says:

> *I have been young, and now am old; yet have I not seen the righteous forsaken, nor his seed begging bread.* Psalm 37:25

God is a God of more than enough, and every one of His promises is mine.

I'M STILL STANDING

At one point, Grady began calling me some two hundred times a day, and this went on for six months or more. It was so trying that I really wanted to change my name from Mama. At the time, Edward Terry was Grady's morning caregiver, and he was very good at it. If Grady had wet the bed, Edward put him in the tub and give him a bath. When it was time to get out, if Grady didn't want to get out, he would go into a rage and literally rip Terry's clothes off of him. I thank God for Terry's patience and endurance. He helped me in this way for nearly two years. God will give you favor too.

Edward took Grady for a ride one morning and had to call me to say that he was parked on the side of the road. Grady had flown into another of his rages. Edward had made the mistake of uttering a word I had specifically warned him never to say. IT was the word *no*. To Grady, *no* meant NEVER, and it infuriated him anytime he heard it. He had asked for some Bojangles' chicken, and Edward had said no. I had taught my sons to always tell Grady, "We'll get it later," but then to make sure later eventually came.

Edward saw what was happening and slowed the car down, but no sooner had he stopped than Grady bolted from the car and took off running. Unable to catch Grady on foot, Edward had to follow him in the car. When he caught up with Grady, he found him in a terrible rage.

Fortunately I had trained Edward how to handle Grady when he was out of control, and he followed instructions. Then, after Grady had calmed down, Edward put him back in the car. I asked him to drive slowly and bring Grady straight home. They made it home safely and without further incident.

Next Grady began hitting himself in the head so violently that we had to make him wear a helmet for protection. Over and over again, he would hit himself in the head, and this was happening about ten times a day. The helmet didn't help much. He would just take it off or refuse to put it on in the first place.

It was then that I started using the biblical process known as binding and loosing. God said:

> *And I will give unto thee the keys of the king-*
> *dom of heaven: and whatsoever thou shalt bind*
> *on earth shall be bound in heaven: and whatso-*
> *ever thou shalt loose on earth shall be loosed in*
> *heaven.* Matthew 16:19

This became one of the main scriptures that I used in the process of deliverance. I was determined to continue to stand!

Chapter 13

I Need Your Healing Power, God

HELP ME, GOD!
YOUR TOUCH MEANS SO MUCH

At this point, Grady needed God's touch very badly. He had been potty trained at two, but now, as an adult, he mysteriously started urinating on the floor. It happened several times a week. As soon as he woke up early in the morning, he would go to his favorite spot, in front of the TV in the den, and there he would relieve himself. Why? No one could imagine.

I kept a rug on top of the carpet in the den, and each time he did this I had to pull it up, throw it over the balcony outside, pour hot water and Pine-Sol over it and scrub it thoroughly. And I do mean scrub.

For me, this was a decoration rug, and I loved it, but, for Grady, it became his accident rug. Several mornings each week I would be outside on the balcony between 5:00-6:00 A.M. scrubbing that rug.

It was a nasty job, but somebody had to do it. I didn't complain, but, instead, learned to thank God for everything I was going through. This storm had a purpose, and that purpose would eventually become obvious. In the meantime, I was grateful to God for giving me strength and the ability to care for my son.

Each morning, when it was time for Grady to wash his face, brush his teeth and shave, he would fly into a rage. One minute he would be looking at me, and the next minute he would be hitting me. We never knew when these episodes would come. He could be smiling one minute, and the next he was beating you to the floor. It got to the point that I was actually a little afraid of him for the first time. No one likes to be hit on all day and half of the night.

Being afraid of my own son bothered me, so I began to speak the Word of God over the situation. God said:

> *For God hath not given us the spirit of fear; but*
> *of power and of love, and of a sound mind.*
>
> 2 Timothy 1:7

It was time to prepare myself more fully for battle. For one thing I started using the Word of God, and, since Grady didn't want to wear his helmet, I started using it myself for protection against his blows. And every chance I got, I laid my hands on his belly (where his spirit resides) and spoke the Word of God over him.

He got wise to the helmet and would try to take it off of me. Usually he would succeed, and then he would start pulling my hair, often pulling it out by the roots. Hair would fly everywhere.

I have always had long nails, and after I stopped working I decided to put on artificial nails. Grady noticed them and began pulling them back violently. Blood spurted every which way ... until I had to finally take off the artificial nails and not wear them anymore.

I continued doing spiritual warfare against these attacks, even when I was so tired and sleepy I wondered if I could continue. God has advised us:

> *Put on the whole armor of God, that ye may be*
> *able to stand against the wiles of the devil.*
>
> Ephesians 6:11

With all that we were going through, God's power was always present.

SEEK HIS FACE, NOT HIS HAND

I cried out to God: "God, You are the only one who can take us through this storm. Oh, God, I'm seeking your face, standing in faith for Grady. God, give me more strength so that I can endure to the end of this journey." It was my daily prayer.

One day I decided to take Grady out and test the waters, see how he was doing. We were driving on Parklane Road when I heard the voice of God's Spirit saying, "Slow down and pull over." I was near Columbia Mall, and when I slowed, I noticed that Grady was starting to bite his fingers. That was always a sign that one of his rages was coming on.

He had been doing this now for fifteen years, and

sometimes blood would pour out where he had cut his fingers with his teeth. He always had sores places on most of his fingers. I drove slowly until I could pull into the Columbia Mall parking lot, and just as I did, he started to fight me.

It is not easy to explain how severe these rages were. Grady seemed like a wild man trying to take your life. But my mind was not on myself; I kept thinking about him. I didn't want him to break a window and cut himself, and I definitely didn't want him to get out the car and get hit by another car or perhaps even attack some innocent bystander. I sensed that God was with me and was giving me strength to hold him in the car.

When Grady has one of his rages, he is suddenly three times as strong as a normal person of the same size, and he had well developed muscles. Without God's help, I would not have been able to handle him. He finally calmed down, and I drove very slowly all the way home.

Why were we still going through these things? My faith in God's power to deliver Grady completely was strong, but I sensed that it just wasn't God's time to do the work yet. God was doing to me as Noah had done in Bible days:

After another forty days, Noah opened the window he had made in the boat and released a raven. The bird flew back and forth until the floodwaters on the earth had dried up. He also released a dove to see if the water had receded and it could find dry ground. But the dove could find no place to land because the water still covered the ground. So it returned to the boat, and Noah held out his hand and drew the dove back inside.   Genesis 8:6-9, NLT

Outside our storm, too, was still raging, and the waters were still too high, so God held out His hand, just as Noah had done with the dove, and He returned us to the safety of our home.

I continued to seek God's face, praising His holy name that His hand was there for my protection. What a wonderful God we serve! Yes, wonderful is His name!

I WALK BY FAITH, NOT BY SIGHT

But let him ask in faith, nothing wavering. For he that wavereth is like a wave of the sea driven with the wind and tossed. For let not that man think that he shall receive anything of the Lord.
                                   James 1:6-7

I continued to stand and believe God, for I knew in my heart that nothing was impossible for Him to do—as we stood in faith. I waited for a while before attempting to take Grady out again, just as Noah had done with the dove.

Eventually it was time to test the waters again. The location would be Captain D's Restaurant, and Grady and I would go through their drive-through and order something to eat. It seemed like a very simple task, but it turned out to be far from it.

For some reason, we were told we would have to wait for our food that day, and Grady had no patience for waiting—ever. If something he wanted was not immediately forthcoming, he quickly became angry. I sensed that this could create a serious problem. What should I do?

If I drove off without the food, that would also disturb Grady and be a cause for him doing battle. I decided to park and wait. When I did, Grady took one look at me and, before I knew what was happening, he was all over me. It was noontime, there was lots of traffic on Two Notch Road, and we were parked close to the highway. Whatever happened, I didn't want Grady to get out, run into traffic, and get hit.

As usual, he needed to hit something or some-one until he calmed down, and, as usual, I was his punching bag. He had a very good shot at my face. I needed to do something, but, above all, I kept say-ing to myself, "I can't allow this boy to get out of the car while his rage is at its highest." He would run right into the road because he had no sense of direction when he was upset. I grabbed him and tried to hold him close to me so that he could not get a good swing.

At the same time I was doing this, I was praying. The anointing of God's Spirit could break this yoke. Anytime Grady heard me praying or binding and loosing out loud, his rages became even more severe, so I prayed within myself in order to keep him calm.

We finally received his fish and fries, and he calmed down. I ask God to protect us on our drive home, and He did, just like that dove in the Bible. We had survived another round, and we were back home again. The water was still too high, but my faith was strong:

Faith without works is dead.   James 2:26

When we pulled up at the house, I noticed a lot of my hair on the front seat, and when I got out a bunch of it fell to the ground. The encounter had been so intense that I had not been aware of how much of my hair he had pulled out until now.

We were still not safely inside the house, and I was asking God to please not let Grady take off running. Thankfully, he calmly went inside.

Later, when I saw myself in a mirror, I was shocked. More hair was falling, and my face seemed to be disfigured on one side, as if I had been in a heavy-weight prize fight. Well, I guess I had been. This was the most Grady had damaged me. On another occasion, he had dislocated two of my fingers, but I was not about to give up on this fight. My faith would not waver. I would continue to walk by faith and not by sight!

THIS, TOO, SHALL PASS

I went to wash a comforter and realized that my dryer was broken, so I decided to take the comforter to the laundromat to dry it. It was another journey, another test of Grady's progress. Actually the laundromat was within walking distance of our house, but I couldn't risk Grady getting away, so I would have to drive.

I asked Grady if he wanted to go to the laundromat with me, and, of course, he said he did. We got in the car, and he seemed to be doing fine. We drove up to the laundromat and got out. I couldn't leave Grady in the car by himself, so we went inside together.

I turned to put the comforter in the dryer and when I did, I heard a loud noise. When I turned back, Grady had begun hitting a woman who was there doing her laundry.

"Oh, Lord," I prayed, "I need Your help now."

The lady's hair was standing up on her head, one earring was on the floor, and Grady was ready to tear her head off. I had to physically pull him off of her.

Once the threat was over, I began to apologize for Grady, but the woman was very kind and humble. She had been more concerned about Grady than herself. May God bless that woman more and more. His blessings had been with us through another day and another trial of our faith!

Chapter 14

You Have Not Brought Me This Far to Leave Me Now

I KNOW HELP IS ON THE WAY

I sensed, more than ever before, that everything I and Grady had been going through was not by accident. God had a plan, and I needed to be led by His Spirit. I asked God to bring me through this storm, no matter how hard it would be. I knew that

He was with me. He had said that it wasn't about me, but about Him. And I was willing to let His will be done in me so that I could be a blessing to others.

God continued to show me that I should stand on His Word, speak His Word and walk in faith with demonstration. Also I should praise Him in the midst of the storm. For His part, He was there to guide us, and I was sure that He would never leave us or forsake us. He is our very present help in time of need.

MY CONFIDENCE IS IN YOU, GOD

With all we had been through, God was placing me into a closer relationship with Him. I no longer had any girlfriends to relate to, and when God told me to leave my job and totally trust Him, He also told me to release the man I had been dating. He would give me what was best for me, He promised. He began to move aside anything and everything that could hinder His purpose in my life.

God had placed me on the waters, to go through this turbulent storm, and now He moved everything that was around me that might have taken my focus away from Him. He wanted my total and undivided attention. I was not alone in any sense because I had the greatest Friend in the whole world, my loving Father God, who loves me much more than any friend or any man could.

In the process, I learned that when we go through trials and tribulations, it is that we might discover God's plans for our lives. If we already know His plans, we can avoid some of these tests. But we are strengthened in faith in Him during times of trial. When we endure to the end, we come forth as pure gold. So our trials and tribulations do not harm us. They make us stronger in faith, giving us a closer relationship with God and making us a better Christian. God has taught me His purpose for my life as I have traveled this journey.

At one point, many years ago, an anointed man of God told me that I was about to embark on a journey. Then, on two different occasions, the Lord woke me out of sleep to say to me out loud, "You are going on a journey." I heard it so clearly. And what a journey it has been!

I can relate to Job. His friends, at first at least, didn't understand what was happening in his life. I thank God that I didn't have anyone to answer to and have to explain why God had allowed all of this to happen. I'm not sure what I would have told them.

I have learned that life is not about the creation; it's about the Creator. Our God wants His glory to be manifested, and I, for one, am willing to say, "God, use me for Your glory." I have long wanted God to mold me into His image, so I would think like Christ. After I gave my life to God, I knew that I was bought with a price and no long belonged to myself, but to my heavenly Father who gave His Son Jesus Christ for me. Jesus laid His life down as a ransom for me, so that I could have eternal life.

And still today I want the attributes of Christ in me. I want to walk like Him, talk like Him and, most of all, love like Him. Until this moment, my confidence is in God!

HOLD ON! GOD IS NOT FINISHED WITH YOU YET

But our trials had not ended. One day Grady was in the kitchen eating, and I was in the bedroom. I stepped out of the bedroom to say something to him, and when I looked into his eyes and saw his facial expression, I knew that he was in a rage and that it had escalated to its highest peak. I didn't realize that it could get even worse, but at that moment, Grady was like a bull about to charge, and I knew it was time for me to move fast.

I was standing by my bedroom door, and he was in the kitchen door, and I've never known how he got to my door so fast. I quickly moved into my bedroom to lock the door, but he was already there forcing the door open. I tried, with all my strength, to close it, but it was impossible. He had strength such as I have never encountered in my life.

He got the door open and then started beating me on the head. I turned from him to protect my head, and he beat me in the back, as hard as he could, until I ended up on the floor.

Eventually, Grady calmed down, but later that night, I had a back spasm. When I lay down that night to try to go to sleep, I realized that I was having difficulty moving. My back was seriously injured from the beating. The next day was Sunday, and I wanted to go to church and praise the Lord. I touched my back and prayed for my healing. I was finally able to go to sleep, and when I woke up later in the night, I realized that I was totally healed. I went to church that next morning in my six-inch high-heeled shoes. I was determined to show out, praising my God that He had been my Help in such a time of great need. He is truly Jehovah Rophe!

IT WASN'T EASY, BUT IT WAS WORTH IT

After all of these trials, I can say that Grady is a wonderful loving son and that he truly loves his mother. And the feeling is mutual. I have always given him one hundred percent of me and my love. Adolphus said to me one day, "Grady is so blessed to have you as his mother." Grady is well taken care of in every area of his life. After all, he is a son of the King of king's and Lord of lord's. Our heavenly Father loves us even when we do wrong. He does hate sin, but when we repent of our sins, He loves us in a very special way. And, what is so wonderful, He doesn't remember our sins against us anymore. What an awesome God we serve!

Through the years Grady developed many unusual habits. For one whole year, he would constantly rub his lip. Then he stopped that, and a new habit took form. For many years, he beat his left arm. I tried to keep it wrapped to protect it from this abuse, but he would beat it until the wrapping disintegrated and fell off. After he had hit his head and arm enough times, they became permanently darkened (until he is restored).

During the whole long process of caring for Grady I never let him be an excuse for me not fulfilling my calling. I was called to preach the Good News of the Gospel of Jesus Christ, and I would do that regardless of what happened. I was able to fulfill all of the duties assigned to me in my local church, and, remarkably, most of the people of the church never knew what I had been going through.

When you suffer like Grady has suffered, and you try to explain it to other people, it can be more than they can comprehend. The details of my storm were more than most people could understand, so I just stood in the waves and didn't take my eyes off of Jesus. Only He really knew and understood.

This reminds me of what Peter experienced when he tried to walk to Jesus on the water of the Sea of Galilee (see Matthew 14:29-33). The winds were so boisterous that day that Peter became afraid and began to sink. But Jesus, with much love, showed compassion on Peter, stretching forth His hand to help him in his time of need. That's the God I serve.

One of the callings of my ministry was to write this book and explain what faith can do if we keep our eyes on God and trust Him in all of life's difficulties. God will bring you out of any situation, and He will give you peace and joy while you are going through your particular storms. If we can't trust anyone else on earth, we definitely can trust God in every situation. The enemy fought the writing of this book in so many ways, but it got done and now you are reading the story, and so we are victorious.

Is anything too hard for God? Of course not! He is God!

Whenever God has asked me to do something, I learned to do it and then did it unto Him, all the while trusting Him to intervene in our home situation. Grady's caregivers were among the few who knew just what I was facing on a daily basis. I was sure that God would intervene for us in His time. I just had to learn to work on His time clock and not my own. He said:

> *Trust in the LORD with all thine heart; and lean not unto thine own understanding. In all thy ways acknowledge him, and he shall direct thy paths.* Proverbs 3:5-6

I senses that it was now time to do some serious warfare. I decided to take the helmet off and use spiritual armor instead. From then on, when Grady was having one of his rages, I started speaking in tongues, as God gives the utterance, binding the power of Satan and loosing the power of God. Praise God! All fear was gone, and I was ready to do battle with the enemy. Don't get me wrong. There was nothing easy about it, and it was a nearly daily necessity.

I had learned, many years before to let God work things out. If I could just move out of His way, that would allow Him to work as He willed. He always knows what is best for us. Now I was learning to do this more, as the storm raged around me.

I began locking myself in the room with Grady when he was having his rages and praying, and this started breaking the back of the enemy. I sensed that it was Grady's season for breakthrough and I must do whatever was necessary to get him there.

When I started doing this lock down, Cornelious would just look at me. I could sense that he didn't want me to lock myself in the same room with Grady. He refused to speak negatively to me about it, but I could sense his unease. Still, I knew what I had to do. I would take Grady with me into the bedroom, lock the door and begin to do spiritual warfare for him.

The Bible tells us that we have what we say. In fact, death and life are in the power of the tongue:

> *Death and life are in the power of the tongue:*
> *and they that love it shall eat the fruit thereof.*
>
> Proverbs 18:21

Cornelious' eyes had expressed his misgivings, and what I was about to do was not easy, but I had to walk in my destiny, so it was worth it!

I BELIEVE THE STORM IS PASSING OVER

One day I finally said to the enemy, "It's time for you to pack up and leave. Fear is gone, and I have the power of God over you and also a sound mind. I'm about to take back everything you have stolen from me and my son. This is our season to get it back, so back up now and get thee behind me." Then I started pulling down strongholds.

We have to use the Word of God to fight against Satan. God says:

> *For the weapons of our warfare are not carnal, but mighty through God to the pulling down of strong holds.*   2 Corinthians 10:4

War was raging in my house, and the devil knew it. We tried to be careful never to walk ahead of God, but to be directed by His Spirit. But even when we won a round, Satan was always ready to go one more. He never likes to lose. But I didn't care now what he tried. I knew who I was in Jesus Christ. So I continued to put on my spiritual armor and go forth to battle, and I refused to allow the enemy to stop me. God had helped me pass through the middle of the storm. I knew it through the Spirit, and I knew it because Grady was calming down.

Then one Sunday morning, as I was preparing for church, Grady became angry again and began running through the house in a rage. My neighbors were out in their yard, and they started looking to see what was going on in my house.

I had long ago learned never to put on my accessories until I was on the way out the door because Grady would just rip them off. That morning he was running through the house like someone was chasing him with an ax. I came out of my room to see what was going on and to try to calm him and, in my haste, I slipped on the floor and fell. Grady quickly pounced on me and pushed my face down into the carpet so that I could not breathe. He had my head in a lock, and he was on top of me, and I suddenly felt myself leaving this earth.

I knew it was not my time, so I was not afraid. I still had a great work to do. In my spirit, I cried out to the Lord, "I need You!" And He answered my plea. I was somehow able to move my face just enough to catch some air and say, "The blood of Jesus!" When

I said that, Grady relaxed his grip, jumped up (now very calm) and just stood there looking at me in a strange way. There is power in the blood of Jesus. I was alive and thankful.

When I got up from there, I quickly looked at the clock. I was due to teach the Young Adult Sunday School Class that morning. I had only about ten minutes to get my makeup retouched and get going to the church so that I could be on time. I noticed that there was makeup smeared on my lime green shell top, but I didn't have time to redress, so I just put on a suit jacket over it.

Then I quickly put on my accessories and went out the door to church. The only thing that might indicate to anyone what I had just survived was that the tip of my nose was bleeding.

I suppose some might have called someone else to teach in their place that day, but I didn't do that. I was also expected to start prayer before every Sunday morning service and to open the service itself. When the time came, I was in my place and ready to do my duty, especially to teach my class. Those students were so very special to me. I was not about to fail God and the people of my church. Come what may, I would be in my place to do what God had called me to do. It was another day of victory, a day of praising my God.

His Word declares:

> *From the rising of the sun unto the going down*
> *of the same the LORD's name is to be praised.*
>
> Psalm 113:3

I had a lot to be thankful for that day.

Chapter 15

There's a Blessing on the Other Side of Through

LET HIM WORK IT OUT

As I noted in the last chapter, I had learned, many years before this storm, to let God work things out. I just need to move out of His way and let Him work. He always knows best. I learned to do this even more during the storm.

It was a very important time in Grady's life. Now that he was out of school, I took him off of the many medications he had been taking, and he was now in the hands of the Master and in my hands. Now I couldn't lose with the power God used.

Grady needed the power of healing, and Jesus Christ took care of that on the cross for every person in the whole world who would believe. The Word of God tells us:

> *But he was wounded for our transgressions, he was bruised for our iniquities: the chastisement of our peace was upon him; and with his stripes we are healed.* Isaiah 53:5

One of the stripes Jesus bore on the cross was for the healing of autism. I knew God could do anything but fail, and I knew that faith moved Him in any situation. So, I said to Him now, "Daddy, it's on! Have Your way, God! Grady and I are in Your hands. I prefer that he not take controlled substances. Jesus took enough pain in His body for Grady."

I took the Word of God and spoke it out into the atmosphere: "With the stripes of Jesus Christ, Grady Devon Lee is healed." Words are powerful when we dare to speak them in faith. I was learning to say what Jesus said and not what I saw.

As Grady started calming down, I was able to

speak into his spirit and command it to line it up with the Word of God. I did this because I knew it was Grady's time and season. I started speaking to his mind and calling it healed and whole, with nothing missing and nothing broken. I spoke out that he had peace and the joy of God through our Lord Jesus Christ.

Anytime Grady looked like he didn't have joy I would ask him to leap for joy. The Bible tells us that if we don't have joy we can leap for it. So Grady leaped for joy while God was working it out in him.

HE WAS THERE ALL THE TIME

Grady had stopped smiling around the age of thirteen, but now, at twenty-six, he started smiling again. And what a beautiful smile it was!

What joy it was for me to see that my son had joy again. Oh, praise God!

Whenever I got the chance, I would speak to Grady and say to him things like this: "Grady Devon Lee, you are a man of God, a mighty man of God, a holy and righteous man of God. You are a valiant man. You are a prophet of God. You walk like God, talk like God and act like God."

One of the times I would speak powerful words

like these into his spirit was during his bath time. I didn't always get to oversee his bath because sometimes he had caregivers in to assist him.

One day I asked him at bath time, "Who is Grady Devon Lee?"

His body stiffened, and he stood at attention, under an obvious anointing of the Holy Ghost, "I'm a man of God!"

This shocked me so much that I jumped back. The anointing was just that strong upon him. We know that we will have what we say.

Most people say what they have:

"I'm so sick!"
"I don't have any money."
"I can't make it."

And the list goes on. But God says differently, and His Word can never return void. He was there all the time.

THERE IS PEACE IN THE STORM! BE STILL!

God often used His prophets to give me encouraging words concerning Grady. One day God told me through a prophet, "Man will know, doctors will know, and psychiatrists will know that it was God who delivered thee."

My fate was in God's hands. I learned, through my storm, to glorify Him regardless of the pain or suffering we might presently be enduring. I learned to move with Him and not away from Him. After all, God destined this storm for my life, and it would blow over at His appointed time. In the meantime, I had to continue to flow in the power of the Holy Ghost.

Having gone through all of this, I can say with full assurance, that God will give you peace in the midst of your storm. One day, when Jesus and His disciples were together in a boat crossing the sea, a storm arose:

> *But soon a fierce storm came up. High waves were breaking into the boat, and it began to fill with water. Jesus was sleeping at the back of the boat with his head on a cushion. The disciples woke him up, shouting, "Teacher, don't you care that we're going to drown?"*
>
> *When Jesus woke up, he rebuked the wind and said to the waves, "Silence! Be still!" Suddenly*

the wind stopped, and there was a great calm.
Then he asked them, "Why are you afraid? Do
you still have no faith?" Mark. 4:37-40, NLT

Why was Jesus asleep in that all-important moment? It was because He knew that no weapon formed against Him or His disciples could prosper. Like the disciples that day, I sometimes felt like I was going to drown. (Remember the dream I had going over the bridge.)

In my case too, it definitely seemed like God must be sleeping. But we need to know our heavenly Father better. He never sleeps. He was being still because He knew we would make it through. He knows exactly when to rebuke the storm, and when He does, it will always obey Him.

The disciples marveled at what they saw that day, saying, "Who is this man, that even the wind and waves obey Him?" Everything in Heaven, on Earth and beneath the Earth must obey Him. Therefore we can stand still, even as the tempest rages all around us, for God will give us peace in the midst of the storm.

I NEVER WOULD HAVE MADE IT WITHOUT YOU

One of the reasons I so stubbornly clung to God's

promise for Grady over the years was that I had experienced miraculous healings so many times already, for myself and my other children. Once, when Grady was six and we were still living in Germany, I became very ill. I felt like I was pregnant, but when I went to a doctor there on base, tests showed that I was not pregnant after all, and the doctor was unable to discover why I was feeling so bad.

My marriage ended, and I returned to South Carolina to live with my three sons. With the move and the care of the boys, I didn't take time to go get another examination, but I continued to feel very bad. Then one day, I was out with Uncle Willie and Aunt Louise Brown, and I fainted. They rushed me to the emergency room at Fort Jackson Army Hospital. Willie and Louise noticed that I had lost a lot of weight. It was because I had no appetite, and, what's worse, I would sometimes cough for hours without stopping. The doctors at Fort Jackson called for a complete examination and an x-ray of my chest.

When the x-ray came back, the door was not completely closed, and I was able to look into the adjoining room and see two doctors looking at it together. They would look at the x-ray and then look at each other, and it was not a pleasant look. I knew that something was very wrong.

The doctors came back into my room and asked me if I had ever smoked. I told them no. They sent me the next day to Richland Memorial Hospital to have some more tests done. I wasn't sure what they were going to find, but I knew that I would survive it with God's help.

IT'S MY TIME NOW

While these new tests were being processed, I went home. Eventually a doctor called me to come in and talk over the results. I remember his precise words: "Mrs. Lee, you have a disease known as sarcoidosis, and it has caused the deterioration of the majority of your lungs. Doctors don't know what causes this disease, but it can take many forms and it can be very serious. When it affects the lungs, it becomes life-threatening. Mrs. Lee, you will die if we don't start treatment as soon as possible. We need to airlift you right now to Walter Reed Hospital in Washington, D.C."

I just looked at the doctor in unbelief and said, "But I'm a single mother with three children to raise, and one of my children requires twenty-four hour care. I simply wouldn't be able to go."

He said, "Well, in that case, I will order some

medications for you, and I'll call you as soon as they come in." He told me about the possible side-effects from the medicine and then ended with, "Now if you don't take this medication, you won't survive this disease."

When I walked out of his office that day, my mind was already made up. I would not take the medicine. Instead, I would stand on God's Word, and I started quoting to myself and the devil all that God had promised me.

There were two main scriptures that I stood on and refused to waver from. It was my time for healing, for my life was now on the line.

HE WILL TURN YOUR MIDNIGHT TO DAYLIGHT

At first, as I stood on God's Word, I became worse, but that didn't sway me. I was determined to walk by faith and not by sight. I was well aware of the doctor's word, that sarcoidosis, if left unchecked, could cause a deterioration of various organs of the body, that it could be helped by medications, but that often those medications caused their own complications. But I wanted to work the Word of God and not the medicine. I felt good with my choice.

As time passed I woke up one morning and was totally blind. The eye was one of the organs the doctor had warned me sarcoidosis could affect. I closed my eyes again and started talking to God, and I had a smile on my face. It was a moment I will never forget. I said, "God, I have to see in order to take care of my sons, especially Grady. I trusted You to work this miracle through my faith. I need a right-now blessing, and You are a right-now God."

Often, during His ministry on Earth, Jesus had said: *"Thy faith hath made thee whole"* (Matthew 9:22, Mark 5:34 and 10:52, Luke 8:48 and 17:19). When I opened my eyes, I was able to see again. Faith will move a mountain, and it definitely will move God. I needed provision right at that moment. Not tomorrow, but at that very second. And God was and still is a right-now God.

I didn't tell any other family members what I had been diagnosed with, especially my parents and siblings. Instead, I put my life in the Master's hands. During this time, God sent an anointed woman I had never met before to touch and agree with me. There is power in such agreement. If God sends someone to pray with you, they are definitely living holy.

God had my back again. I don't know anyone on this Earth that loves me like He does. People can often pass you by and never know what you need, but God will stop to help you in your storm. What a Mighty God He is! Jesus said:

> *"I also tell you this: If two of you agree down here on earth concerning anything you ask, my Father in heaven will do it for you."*
>
> Matthew 18:19, NLT

While we are trying to figure things out, God has already worked them out. Thank You, Lord, for daylight!

THE TWO SCRIPTURES I STOOD ON:

The two scriptures I stood on were these:

> *And Jesus answering saith unto them, Have faith in God. For verily I say unto you, That whosoever shall say unto this mountain, Be thou removed, and be thou cast into the sea, and shall not doubt in his heart, but shall believe that those things, which he saith shall come to pass; he shall have whatsoever he saith.*
>
> Mark 11:22-23

But he was wounded for our transgressions, he was bruised for our iniquities: the chastisement of our peace was upon him; and with his stripes we are healed.   Isaiah 53:5

HE CAN HANDLE IT

God gave me a whole new life. About a month later, my appetite had returned, and I started regaining the weight I had lost. I knew that God had healed me with His Word. Eight months later, I returned to the hospital without an appointment. I waited in the waiting room until the doctor was able to see me. When he came to call me to come in, he didn't recognize me. I had gained nearly twenty pounds, so my face was a little fuller.

I just handed him my medical record with a smile, and he said, "Oh, you're not who I thought you were." I stood there in silence waiting for him to open the records. He opened the file and then looked back at me and eventually asked me to come on into the office.

The first question he asked was, "Where have you been? I ordered the medications for you, but then I wasn't able to contact you at the number you left me, so I was worried."

I explained to him that I had moved.

"Well, did you go to another doctor?" he asked.

"No," I answered.

He looked at me quizzically. Then it was my turn to ask a question. "Do you believe in God?"

"Yes," he said, "as a matter of fact, I do."

"Well," I told him, "I didn't take any medications. I just worked the Word of God through faith, and God totally healed me."

"Well, I would like to examine you again," he said. "It's not that I don't believe you, but it would be good to be sure." I agreed.

He listened to my lungs, and told me they sounded strong.

"Would you mind having another x-ray?" he asked. "That would tell us for sure, one way or the other."

I told him I didn't mind, so I went and had an x-ray taken, then I waited while they processed the film, and I brought it back to the doctor without looking at it. I didn't need to look. I knew what it showed.

The doctor took the x-ray out of its envelope, placed it on the screen for viewing and turned the light on. It was a moment to be remembered for a lifetime. Praise God, He had given me two new lungs.

This doctor was the head over Internal Medicine at Fort Jackson Hospital at the time. Once he saw the x-ray proof of my healing, we then had a long conversation concerning the power of God and how He does miracles. He told me he had never had a patient who had stood on the Word of God alone and received their healing, although he did have patients who had used prayer and medication together. I never went back to him, for I never needed to. God had totally healed me, and the problem never reoccurred.

Doctors and medications are not evil, but even with doctors and medications, we must stand in God, praying and believing Him to use the doctors and the mediations to cure our sicknesses, diseases or infirmities. And God can do it alone. With Him, we just need to have faith and stand on His Word.

Just this week a nurse said to me, "We all have to die from something." I felt that God wanted me to enlighten her from His Word. As kindly as possible, I let her know that what she had said was not scriptural and that God had ways of healing us from any and every disease. I thank God for allowing my doctor to recognize that His power is greater than all medications.

It has been twenty-two years now, and I am still

totally healed from sarcoidosis. I have not had any more complications with my lungs. Thank God for His healing power!

A friend of mine from high school died about thirteen years ago from the same disease, and she was on medications. I was able to share my testimony with many of how Satan tried to take my life to prevent my destiny and that of Grady from being fulfilled. I had become ill just before returning to this country to dedicate myself more to his care. I cannot fail to give Him praise for healing me. Hallelujah! He handled it!

If God could heal me of sarcoidosis, he could heal Grady of autism.

Chapter 16

Glory to the Lamb of God

LAY YOUR BURDENS AT HIS FEET

God continued to bless us, just like the loving Father he is. His arms are never too short to bless, and His heart is full of enough love to go around the world and back again. I have been on the battlefield for many years, but God has not felled me yet. And guess what: He never will.

Grady had a doctor's appointment with Dr. Malone and, for the first time, I decided to take him without one of his brothers along to serve as "bodyguard." When we walked into the doctor's office, I asked him if he noticed anything different. It took him a few seconds to realize that no other son was with us to help control Grady. Through many transitions, Dr. Malone had seen the power of God at work in Grady's life, and this was another milestone. God was taking Grady from glory to glory.

Our visit to the doctor went so well that I decided to take another very big step, something I had not dared to do without someone else present to serve as "bodyguard" since the many rages had started. I dressed my handsome son and took him out to dinner.

"Here we go again," my mind was shouting, and this time I was taking him out to the Columbia Mall, the very place he had experienced the rage that infamous 4th of July and the same mall he had run through in a great rage with his brother chasing behind. I needed to exercise my faith in God, or I might just regret this decision.

I had already prayed over Grady, speaking God's Word into his spirit, and now I was standing in faith for what God had promise. God had begun breaking down walls, destroying yokes and uprooting wrong foundations, so that we were now able to see the manifestation of His power, taking Grady from glory to glory. This was another important step in the process.

IF THE LORD NEVER DOES ANYTHING ELSE FOR ME, HE HAS DONE ENOUGH ALREADY

There were several challenges. I decided to go around lunchtime (when the mall was very busy). and I would have to take Grady upstairs to one of the restaurants, and they would be very crowded. Worst of all, Grady had always been very fearful of riding the escalator. This day was to be different. We were going to the mall in God's timing and for His glory, and we would have a safe trip. I knew it.

When we arrived at the mall, we got inside without incidence. This was such a monumental experience and I was so happy about what was happening that I wanted to share it with someone. I decided to call Adolphus and tell him. As we were walking through the mall, I called him and said, "Hi, Adolphus, guess where your mother and Grady are today?"

He couldn't have guessed in a million years.

I continued, "We're at Columbia Mall."

He said, "What? Mama!" And then he became

very quiet. A good son, he had been taught about the power of the tongue, and he was not about to say anything negative. But his silence said it all. Fear had gripped him because of his love for me.

I said, "We're going upstairs, and we're going to sit down, and we're going to eat." I had already made up my mind that I would not order our food and then be forced to leave before it came because of Grady's actions. I wanted to see God's glory manifested in an impossible situation.

Adolphus was still so quiet on the other end that I was wondering if he had dropped the phone. "Well, I'll talk to you later," I concluded.

He answered rather solemnly, "Okay, Mama."

I still felt his fear and could imagine what he was thinking: "What is Mama thinking! Grady could have a severe rage and attack someone or even several people. Suppose he falls over the railing when he starts running. Oh, God, is she crazy?"

We got on the escalator and rode to the top with no problem. Now we were upstairs with the huge crowds and all the restaurants were right in front of us. So far, so good. What a blessing to see God's supernatural power at work!

I asked Grady to pick the restaurant he wanted. He chose Chinese food, and we moved toward the Chinese counter.

Then, suddenly, Grady looked around and noticed the large crowd. I was holding him by his hand, and I felt his body start vibrating. Then, suddenly, he let out a loud scream, so loud that it could be characterized as piercing. Everyone around us stopped to look, some with great fear on their faces. I'm sure they must have been wondering if their lives were in jeopardy. But, no, it was just Grady feeling the glory of God. He smiled and was just fine.

We ordered his food and then we sat together at one of the public tables there in the food court and ate. At least I did. Grady was very excited, so excited that he only nibbled at his food and spent his time watching the people around us. But he did this with great peace. It had been years since Grady had sat down at a public restaurant. What a great victory!

When we had finished eating, we walked back through the mall, got safely to our car and went back home, all without incidence. Praise God! Faith moves Him. He had blessed us with a glorious day.

I HAVE BEEN RESTORED

We were on cloud nine because God had showed up and showed out at the Columbia Mall, but my Daddy (God) didn't stop there. I decided to take

Grady with me to Wal-Mart for grocery shopping on a Friday evening. I had him push the buggy for me, and we stayed in the store for a while. He was so quiet I almost forgot he was with me. We purchased the groceries we needed, left peacefully and returned home in safety with no unwanted incidents. From that time on, grocery shopping became one of Grady's assigned (and beloved) tasks.

I had always kept Dr. Malone, Grady's physician, informed of his advancements, and I couldn't wait to give him these two great testimonies. He was shocked and very happy for Grady. He said he remembered days when Grady would come into the waiting room in a great rage. "An autistic person who is not on medication cannot stand to be around crowds of people," he told us. "And Grady is not on medication." I loved the fact that three times in his narrative, he said, "but God," and I, too, knew that God was the answer. To myself, I said, "The Father, the Son, and the Holy Ghost!"

HIS PRESENCE IS ALWAYS THERE

One night I was in the presence of God, reading His Word, and I noticed that the words on the page seemed to be coming together and moving, and they were illuminated. I took off my glasses, but the words continued to move. Then I looked to my left and saw an angel. Full of light, he was moving through my room.

Grady came into the bedroom, but he clearly didn't see the angel, for he walked right toward him to go to the bathroom, so the angel moved out of Grady's way. I watched the angel until I was no longer able to see him. I believed that God had opened my spiritual eyes to see Grady's guardian angel, sent to protects him in every situation.

On July 20 of 2010, I had a very special dream. I took Grady to a physician I had never seen in my life. I can remember him still, with his white jacket on and holding Grady by one hand. I had Grady's other hand. The doctor was pulling us both from one office to another. I noticed that the top of Grady's hair was blonde and had a bright golden glow about it. I couldn't take my eyes off of it. Then I heard a lady saying that this doctor was such a good man and had a very kind spirit. When I awoke I knew that it had been a dream from God.

Through prayer God revealed to me what the dream meant. He said to me, "The doctor was the Great Physician, My Son, Jesus Christ. The boy's hair was golden because he has been through the storm and is now coming out as pure gold. Jesus was holding Grady and you by the hand because it is your time to come out of the storm. He, Jesus, the Great Physician, is bringing you out."

I answered, "Praise God! Jesus is indeed the Great Physician (Jehovah Rophe)."

WORTHY IS THE LAMB OF GOD WHO PROTECTED US IN THE STORM

I want to give praises to You, Most His God and to the Lamb, for bringing us through this storm. My Lamb of God, You have changed my life. You are my Savior. You are my Rose of Sharon and my Lily of the Valley. You are my Wheel in the middle of the wheel. You are my Shepherd, and I shall not want. You are my Redeemer and my Defense. You are my Rock, my Fortress, and my Deliverer; my God, my Strength, in whom I will trust; my Buckler, and the Horn of my Salvation, and my High tower. You are my King of king's and my Lord of lord's!

I praise my holy God because He was there every hour, minute and second to protect Grady and me in the storm. His arms were not too short to hold me by my hand. He covered me with His protection. When I lost sense of direction, He reached His hand out to guide my path. The Lamb of God has been my strength. Oh, God, what I would have done without You? I have really learned to lean on You. Every day was not easy, but it was worth it. You didn't allow the hurricane to take me under. The thunder came, the lightning and the waves of the storm, but, God, you were there to protect Grady and me.

My storm lasted for many years, and I asked You to take me through it, I have been a willing vessel. I didn't dictate any particular length of time. I just trusted You, for I wanted Your will to be done in my life. I knew what Your Word said:

> *But, beloved, be not ignorant of this one thing, that one day is with the Lord as a thousand years, and a thousand years as one day.*
>
> 2 Peter 3:8

So everything was in Your hands. I just wanted You to use me for Your glory.

Finally, I want to report that I am now in the process of getting Grady prepared for ministry. This is his time and his season. When Moses was born to a Hebrew woman in slavery in Egypt, she recognized him as a prophet of the Most High and placed him in a basket and laid it among the reeds along the edge of the Nile River to save his life. Pharaoh's daughter found the child and had compassion on him. She needed someone to nurse him, so Moses' sister went to get her mother (also Moses' mother), and she was given the privilege. Look at how God works! As the child grew, she brought him to Pharaoh's daughter, and he became her son.

Sometimes a mother's heart carries great pain because she does not yet know all the plans of God, but Moses became one of the greatest prophets in the Old Testament and was used to help deliver the Israelites out of bondage.

To every reader of this book, I want to say, Look beyond your pain and suffering, for God is trying to take you to another level in Him. He did it for Moses, and He is the same God today.

A mother's pain can birth you into your destiny, if she can see who you are in Christ Jesus. Oh, believe me, I knew who Grady was in Christ. He has long been called to be a great prophet of the Lord. After many years of birthing, suffering, and enduring, many years of trusting God, many years of praying, many years of waiting upon God to say, "Okay, it's his season now," I can say that it was all worthwhile.

I always knew that faith could move God, and I

made up my mind that the devil would not win this battle. I just had to stay in the race and believe that my God was able to bring Grady out:

> *Trust in the* Lord *with all thine heart; and lean not unto thine own understanding. In all thy ways acknowledge him, and he shall direct thy paths.*   Proverbs 3:5-6

There is greatness in all of us, but we must allow God to bring it to the surface. There is never a shortage in God's power; the only shortage is in our faith. There are many different levels of faith, and each of us needs to build his or her faith until it can be described as great faith.

Jesus is the Great Physician, and I know that with the stripes of Jesus Christ, Grady is healed. One of Jesus' stripes was for autism, and nothing is impossible for God to do—if we can only believe Him.

We must have faith in God for every situation. We need to trust Him for our finances because He is our Provider (Jehovah Jireh), for our healing, because He is the Healer (Jehovah Rophe); and when we need God to be there to lift our spirits, He is our Peace (Jehovah Shalom).

If you are a born-again Christian, don't let anyone tell you that medicine is your only hope for healing. Build your faith in God, trusting that He has all power. By the stripes of Jesus Christ you are healed already. Activate your faith by working on it with love.

When He was here, walking on Earth, Jesus said:

> *Thou shalt love the Lord thy God with all thy heart, and with all thy soul, and with all thy mind. This is the first and great commandment. And the second is like unto it, Thou shalt love thy neighbour as thyself. On these two commandments hang all the law and the prophets.*
> Matthew 22:37-40

God spoke through me one day, as I was ministering to someone, and said: "My people don't have great faith because they don't love Me." We first have to fall in love with God. Lose all self-ambition and get lost in His Spirit. Then we need to be obedient to God in everything and give Him our whole heart, soul, and mind. Only then can we love everyone else as we should, even our enemies.

When we learn to keep this, the Greatest Commandment, the Word of God will work in every aspect of our lives. Our Faith will be great in God, and there will not be anything impossible for God to do for us.

God released this revelation to me in January of 2010. Then, in October of that same year, I heard a great man of God from Atlanta, Georgia, saying that the first and second commandments govern faith, prayer, love and every other area of our lives. Satan will try to keep us from walking in love with God and people, because that is where your faith works best. If we want the Word of God to work in its fullness in our lives, we must first become obedient to the Great Commandment. This is divine order from God. We first have to hear what He has asked us to do. Then, as we obey God, by keeping this Great Commandment, He will work for us.

> *So then faith cometh by hearing, and hearing by the word of God.*   Romans 10:17

I insist on walking in the promises of God and rejecting the doubts of man. God is our Solid Rock, and we shall not be moved. Stand, my sisters and brothers, on every promise that God has given. Hold on to your faith and don't let go. What God promises He is more than able to perform. He said:

Looking unto Jesus the author and finisher of our faith; who for the joy that was set before him endured the cross, despising the shame and is set down at the right hand of the throne of God.
Hebrews 12:2

No book, however long, could contain every detail of Grady's life. I have chosen some of the highlights to show how God has been with us in this storm, and there will be more testimonies to comes. God is never late to accomplish His mission. Rather, He is always on time. Through every storm, I chose to press toward the mark for the prize of the high calling of God in Christ Jesus, and I praise God for the Lamb of God!

IN HIS GLORY, I LEARNED TO LEAN ON GOD!

AND YOU CAN TOO. VICTORY IS YOURS!

Trust in Him at all times; ye people, pour out your heart before Him: God is a refuge for us.
Psalm 62:8

MAY GOD BLESS THE READERS OF THIS BOOK!

AMEN!!

A Prayer for Salvation

God has promised:

That if thou shalt confess with thy mouth the Lord Jesus, and shalt believe in thine heart that God hath raised him from the dead, thou shalt be saved. For with the heart man believeth unto righteousness; and with the mouth confession is made unto salvation. Romans 10:9-10

If you would like to receive Jesus as your Savior, pray out loud the following prayer:

Heavenly Father, I come to You now. I acknowledge You as God, Creator of Heaven and Earth.

Heavenly Father, I confess that I am a sinner and I ask for Your forgiveness. I turn from my sins and choose You to be the Lord of my life and to lead me in all areas of my life. I believe, heavenly Father, that Jesus is alive and seated at Your right hand in Heaven. I receive You, Lord Jesus, as my Lord and Savior with all my heart and believe that You are my King and My God.

Thank You, heavenly Father, for my salvation by faith in Christ Jesus and the truth of Your Word.

In Jesus' name,
Amen!

Ministry Page

Readers may contact Minister Patricia A. Lee at the following addresses:

IN ALL GOD'S GLORY MINISTRY
Minister/Prophetess Patricia A. Lee
P.O. Box 291601
Columbia SC 29229

www.PatriciaALee.org